The Asperger Parent

How to Raise a Child with Asperger Syndrome and Maintain Your Sense of Humor

Jeffrey Cohen

Foreword by Lori Shery

Autism Asperger Publishing Company
P.O. Box 23173
Shawnee Mission, Kansas 66283-0173
www.asperger.net

©2002 by Autism Asperger Publishing Co.
P.O. Box 23173
Shawnee Mission, Kansas 66283-0173
www.asperger.net

Publisher's Cataloging-in-Publication
(provided by Quality Books, Inc.)

Cohen, Jeffrey N.
    The Asperger parent : how to raise a child with
Asperger syndrome and maintain your sense of humor /
Jefferey N. Cohen ; with foreword by Lori Shery.
    p. cm.
    Library of Congress Control Number: 2002111902
    ISBN: 1-931282-14-5

    1. Asperger's syndrome–Popular works. 2. Parenting.
3. Child rearing. 4. Asperger's syndrome–Patients–
Family relationships. 5. Parents of autistic children.
6. Autistic children–Care I. Title.

RJ506.A9C64 2002   649'.154
                          QBI02-200638

This book is designed in Rage Italic and Berkeley

Managing Editor: Kirsten McBride
Cover and Interior Design: Tappan Design

Dedication

This book is for Joshua,
who is an endless source of pride,
awe and inspiration,
even on the days when
he's driving me especially crazy.

Acknowledgments

This book wouldn't have been remotely possible without any of the people who submitted for interviews, whom I have listed in the Notes. They and the other Asperger parents I spoke with, some of whom asked not to be identified, are the heroes and heroines of this book, along with the children of whom they are so justifiably proud.

I'd like to thank my own family: my wife, my daughter Eve, and naturally Josh, for letting me tell our story, since the story wouldn't be right without any one of them present. I hope the intrusions into our privacy weren't too deep and that they realize our experiences are universal, which was the point of this book. Thanks to my mother and brother, for wanting so badly to know what this Asperger thing was, and what they could do to help. They continue to be enormously helpful to this day.

Thanks, too, to Kirsten McBride, for editing so unobtrusively and letting me be as idiosyncratic as I wanted; this is not your typical autism book, and she responded so enthusiastically that it pushed me along. Same said about Keith Myles, who responded to my strange idea in the first place.

While I'm in thanking mode, more than a little appreciation is due to Mrs. Joyce Gregus, who has guided my son and his AS through four years (so far) of school so smoothly and thoughtfully; to the teachers, principals and professionals in the Irving Primary and Bartle Elementary Schools in Highland Park, New Jersey; and hopefully to those who are about to meet Josh, in the middle school and high school in that same school system. They have never caused me to consider going in with "guns a-blazing," and for that I am extremely grateful.

To all Asperger parents and their children: keep up the good work; it really does pay off as you go along.

– *Jeffrey Cohen*
July 2002

Foreword

When my son Adam was diagnosed with Asperger Syndrome at age nine, I felt a mixture of relief at finally having a diagnosis and a sense of isolation because I knew of no other parents who had a child with this disorder.

In order to effectively parent and advocate for our special children, we need to have a support system in place for ourselves. Having a loving family and a close circle of friends is crucial, but it's not enough.

The support of parents in the same circumstances is invaluable. When they say they know what we are going through, they do! Another parent can help us get through the most difficult times with words of wisdom from someone who has "been there, done that." There is great comfort in knowing we are not alone.

Not everyone is able to get to a parent support meeting. Jeff Cohen has done an outstanding job of bringing such a group directly to us, suggesting that we think of this book as "a support group you can take with you wherever you go." It is that and much more.

First, we meet his son Josh. We are given a glimpse into the author's daily existence, and we understand his motivation for writing this book.

Next, he introduces us to others we can identify with. There are interviews with parents – married, single, those with young children, those with teenagers, and those with adult children, parents who run support groups and parents who act as advocates for others. As we read their first-person accounts, we find ourselves nodding our heads in understanding. Someone else actually says the same awful things we say in a moment of anger! There really are other parents who cry themselves to sleep at night! We are not the only ones who make stupid mistakes and walk around feeling guilty afterwards! There are quotes from psychologists, school special services directors, and camp directors. We learn that it's okay to be human and to forgive ourselves for not being perfect.

Just as importantly, we are reminded to tend to the other relationships in our lives. We are not defined solely by our roles as parents of a child with special needs. We are so much more, and we need to be mindful of that.

A support group wouldn't be helpful without offering plenty of practical suggestions to choose from. And there are many to be found in this "portable" version. From ignoring the disapproving stares of onlookers in the mall, to disclosure of our child's disability, training of school staff, sibling issues, maintaining one's sanity throughout the teenage years, to post-high school education and employment issues and beyond, this book offers something for everyone.

Throughout, Jeff encourages us to view life with a healthy dose of humor. Don't sweat the small stuff. But do laugh at the funny stuff. A good hearty laugh. Some of it is hysterical. And remember to appreciate our children's every accomplishment, no matter how seemingly insignificant. For them, there are no small victories.

> *– Lori S. Shery*
> *President, Co-Founder*
> *ASPEN, Inc.*

Why This Book Isn't About Your Child

$\mathcal{E}$VERY ONE OF US HAS A STORY.
In 1991, my son Joshua, who was then two years old, was thrown out of his first nursery school. He had been biting other children (Josh has a talent for finding the mode of behavior that is least socially acceptable), and no matter what punishments he faced, he continued to do so when he thought someone had broken a rule – any rule. Finally, the school couldn't take it anymore.

The following year, around the time his sister was being born, Josh was asked to leave a second nursery school: same problem, same solution. No matter how carefully the situation was explained to Josh, he continued to "mete out justice" in the way he'd chosen. He didn't seem able to control himself, and rarely even appeared to be listening when we'd explain the error in his ways. This might have been the first time we noticed he didn't often make eye contact.

1

The second nursery school, after asking us to withdraw Josh, suggested we contact a child psychologist. The teacher had noticed something she considered familiar; her twelve-year-old daughter still had what the teacher called "hissy fits." We talked to our pediatrician, and he recommended a doctor he knew.

Josh was having problems going to sleep at night. He had refused to get into a crib pretty much from his second birthday, and was now claiming his bedroom was infested with crocodiles. He would scream, even with a nightlight, that it was too dark in the room. The crocodiles would get him.

About the same time, he had started cutting back on the range of foods he would consent to eat. A boy who at one time would eat virtually anything presented to him was down to three choices for any given meal: pasta, hot dogs or macaroni and cheese – which is really two choices. And each had to be prepared in the same way every time, or it would be refused.

The child psychologist tested Josh and recommended some behavior modification techniques. We were able to get Josh to go to sleep in his room at night, after some horrific evenings spent listening to him wail in terror through a closed bedroom door. That was the extent to which behavior modification worked. We didn't have the heart to try it again.

At four, Josh was registered in a pre-kindergarten for "handicapped" children run by the town we were living in at the time. The speech therapist there suggested his problem was one of auditory processing; Joshua wasn't absorbing everything that was said to him. So Josh began speech therapy on a daily basis.

Not long after that, we spoke to another psychologist, who told us, after considerable testing, that Josh was, and always would be, "eccentric." I told him we didn't have enough money for Josh to be eccentric; the best we could afford was neurotic. Strangely, the doctor didn't find that comment amusing.

Finally, after a stop in another pre-K for children with disabilities (where we were told to take Josh home because there was "no problem at all that we can see"), our son started kindergarten.

Two weeks into the term, the teacher asked to see us. She had noticed him flapping his hands and staring at the ceiling when the other kids were playing. She had also noted his refusal to sit on certain areas of the rug that were scratchier than others. She thought he wasn't ready to start school.

Luckily, the school system in our town was flexible. Josh stayed in kindergarten, and the child study team – which included a psychologist, an educational consultant, his teacher, a social worker and a case manager – tested him in any number of different areas. And after all that, it was suggested he see a pediatric neurologist.

My wife had done some research, so when we went to the neurologist, she already had a suspicion what the diagnosis would be. Not surprisingly, the neurologist came up with exactly the words she expected to hear.

Asperger Syndrome.

In 1995, when Joshua was (finally) diagnosed with Asperger Syndrome (AS), my wife and I felt a rush of conflicting emotions: relief, that we knew what we were dealing with; wonder, since we didn't *really* know yet what we were dealing with; trepidation, because the rest of the world surely hadn't heard of what was then an esoteric condition; worry, because there didn't seem to be anyone else we could talk to about Josh who would really understand. And fear, because it was a lifelong condition with no cure.

Thank goodness there was Lori Shery.

At just about the moment Josh was halfway through first grade, Lori, who lives one town north of us, was creating ASPEN, the Asperger Syndrome Education Network, and holding her first support group meetings in a building perhaps fifteen minutes by car from my house. That is a stroke of luck one can't ever hope to duplicate.

Lori's own son Adam is about three years older than Josh, and she had been dealing with AS longer than we had, even before we knew the disorder had a name. She had been nagging

3

doctors, badgering teachers, perplexing principals and petitioning school boards for quite some time, and knew the ropes.

She's also one of the four most selfless people on the planet, so she was offering to help those who, like us, knew the name of the condition but not what to do about it. And she was organizing parents like us to get together once a month, tell our stories, ask each other questions, and just plain *commiserate*. Local newsletters were including notices about the meetings, and other organizations were also mentioning ASPEN in their newsletters, so my wife found out about the meetings. If you needed a shoulder to cry on, Lori would provide fifty or sixty people (that's up to 120 shoulders).

I attended a number of the meetings that first year, after my wife had attended some on her own (one of us had to stay home with the kids). After one or two, I was a "veteran," since nobody had any experience in AS at the time, and I soon came to learn how to recognize the "rookies," people whose children had just been diagnosed, who had just heard the words "Asperger Syndrome," or, more scary, "autism" for the first time, and were there to explore the waters of parent support.

You could tell them by the glazed expression in their eyes, as if they'd taken a strong dose of codeine-laced cough syrup and were not exactly living in the same time zone as the rest of us. You could see the tight-lipped, forced smiles when they walked in, wondering if the other parents would understand, or think they were "failures," or "bad parents" for not being able to cope as easily with AS as TV parents did with their problem of the week, always solved in twenty-two minutes or less. You could feel the tension in a handshake, hear the anxiety in the questioning voices. You could see the strain around the eyes and the tightness around the mouth.

And that was on the good nights.

If you went to enough meetings, though, and you saw the rookies become vets, you saw the change, the transformation: the worry didn't go away, but the tension did. Smiles became less forced. They started answering, instead of asking, questions. They spoke confidently about working with school systems, finding day care options, medicating or not medicating. Instead of floating out feelers to see if it was "all right," they offered opinions.

The difference wasn't the expert advice being offered or the chocolate donuts at the back of the room (although both were excellent). What happened to these parents was a natural outgrowth of their exposure to other parents who were in the same situation and *understood*. It was like being dropped into a foreign country and finding someone who speaks your language. Not having to explain every nuance of your problem, not having to hold back information for fear it would be misinterpreted, not having to worry that you were being judged; all these were components in the growth of confidence in these new AS parents. Getting through half a sentence and seeing the person you're talking to nod his head in recognition can be a powerful moment when you're trying to navigate through unknown territory.

AS is a nebulous condition; it's hard to pin down. The child usually isn't outwardly "different;" in fact, most adults who meet a child with AS probably wouldn't notice anything unusual for a few minutes, depending on the child's age. And even when a tic or an inability to make eye contact is noted, it's still hard to explain exactly what AS is all about. Many parents of children who don't have the condition think we are being overly sensitive, that we're coddling our kids, or that we're just plain wrong. There's nothing wrong with our children that *they* can see.

Because of this distinction, finding parents who have had the same experiences, and therefore "get" what you're talking about, can be invaluable to the sanity of an AS parent. So a support group met all sorts of needs for my wife and me in 1997, and we still rely on some of the people we met (chiefly Lori) when we have a question or just need to vent.

Not everybody has a support group, though. That's why this book is not about your child. It's about you.

5

Since AS has become more "mainstream" in the past ten years or so, since people have started hearing about it, since it became listed in medical indexes, a good number of books have been published on how to help a child who has AS. Many of them are very good, and quite helpful. And it is right that most of the focus be concentrated on the people with AS, particularly on the children, and how we can help them live better lives and maximize their gifts and talents. That's absolutely the way things should be.

BUT. That doesn't mean we, as parents, should ignore our own needs entirely. We aren't just the parents of a child with AS; we're also men and women, husbands and wives, brothers and sisters, sons and daughters. We're lawyers and writers and sales-people and mechanics. We're lovers and sports fans. And we're the mothers and fathers of siblings who may be neurotypical.

So far, there hasn't been much written on the needs of parents who deal with AS every day. What to do on those nights when it feels like you just can't handle another ten minutes. When you want to talk to your child about something other than the flight patterns of Canadian geese during the month of November. When another parent touches you pityingly on the arm and asks how your child *really* is doing these days. When the school system suggests either that you're imagining a problem, since the test scores are fine, or that the problem is far more serious than you think, and your child should not be included with the other students his age.

In other words, think of this book as a support group you can take with you wherever you go.

I'm not setting myself up as an expert on AS; I'm not a doctor, a researcher, a sociologist, a psychologist or a social worker. I'm not an educational consultant who can help you through a school system. I'm not qualified to tell you if your child should take medication and, if so, what kind, if it will have side effects or if it will benefit your child in any way. I wouldn't presume for one second to tell you how to raise your child.

What I am is another parent whose child is dealing with AS. I've been living with the condition for more than thirteen years by the time you read this, and dealing with it by name for more than eight. I have contended with many of the situations that you will face, if your child is very young, or have faced, if your child is older. In some cases, I have dealt with the condition brilliantly, coming up with solutions to problems on the fly, improvising my way through tantrums, problems and puzzles. At other times, I've failed miserably, throwing my own tantrums when I reached the end of my rope and let go. I've made hideous mistakes and had glorious victories. I've met other parents in similar situations, and they've told me their stories.

I've been blessed with a wonderful, understanding wife who is the other half of our AS team, just as active a participant in the process as I am, although she goes to an office every day while I sit at home and type. But I know single parents who aren't so lucky. The school system in my town has been very accommodating, but I know parents whose schools have been adversarial and damaging. My wife and I have been very "public" about our son's AS, but we know parents who prefer not to talk about their children's challenges, and we understand that position, too. We give our son medication, but others don't. Either way can work; it depends on the child.

This book is meant to examine what it's like to be the parent of a child with AS: where the pitfalls are, and how to do your best to avoid them. Guilt, and why you shouldn't feel any. Mistakes, and how you'll make some even though you've read this book and found out which ones are most common. How to forgive yourself for the mistakes you are bound to make. Why you shouldn't lose sight of yourself, even as your role of "Mom" or "Dad" seems to overwhelm all the other roles you play.

In these pages, you can find suggestions. Not answers, since everyone has different answers. But those of us who have experienced this condition for long enough have a wealth of suggestions for you to choose from. Try some. If they don't work for you, try others. Remember, we're *all* making it up as we go along; the sociologist Alvin Toffler once said that "parenthood remains the greatest single preserve of the amateur."

Of course, Toffler hadn't met any parents of children with AS when he said that, or didn't know if he had. Otherwise, he might have quoted Wilhelm Busch, who said, "becoming a father is easy enough, but being one can be rough."

Other Parents Think I'm a Monster

I DON'T REMEMBER WHAT IT WAS ANY-
more; something Josh had done just put me over the edge. But I
can tell you exactly what the circumstances were. He was maybe
six years old, and my wife and I, along with his three-year-old
sister Eve, were accompanying Josh on a trip to the Museum of
Natural History in New York, not terribly far from where we live.
It had been a long day, we'd had to fight crowds, the dinosaur
exhibit was impressive to us (but not to the kids) and parking
was costing us upwards of twenty dollars. We had arranged to
meet friends who have children almost exactly the same ages as
ours at the museum, and now everybody was exhausted, heading
back to the parking garage to start the trip home.

To this day, I can place myself in that scene: we were on
West 86th Street, heading west. Josh was sitting on my shoulders, my wife and daughter behind us. The other couple, along

9

with their son, were walking beside me, and their daughter was with my daughter.

Suddenly something Josh did – or said – was the last straw for me.

He had been in a mood all day, one in which nothing would please him. If the french fries in the museum's cafeteria were acceptable, the ketchup wasn't. If he liked the Eskimo exhibit, he was sure to be bored to tears by the giant whale. And now, sitting on my shoulders, he had complained for the 4,000th time of the day, and my limit was 3,999. It wasn't anything that would have upset me at any other time, under any other circumstance. But at that moment, having been worn down all day, it was just enough.

I pulled him down off my shoulders and started to raise my voice, but he wasn't looking at me. So I put my hands on either side of his head and turned it, not hard, so it wouldn't hurt him, but enough to force him to make eye contact with me. And I must have been red in the face as I screamed whatever it was I was trying communicate directly into his face.

At that moment, I turned, and saw our friends staring at me in horror. We hadn't known them very long, and hadn't had the chance to adequately explain AS to them, but they knew Josh has a neurological condition that affects his behavior. It was *my* behavior they couldn't understand. And for a few moments, I saw what had happened through their eyes, and I was just as appalled at myself.

Being an Asperger parent has a good deal to do with patience, a virtue of which I am in lamentably short supply. I do my best, but there are times when I lose perspective. I'm a screamer. Luckily, my children know that after I'm done screaming, I'll come over and apologize and everything will be forgiven on all sides.

But other adults, especially other parents, do not always understand. It seems sometimes that there are two types of adults who are not AS parents: the ones who think you're an evil monster, and the ones who think you're such a softie you can't keep order with your own offspring. In either case, it's hard for parents of AS children to shake the feeling that they're always being judged, and usually being judged as inadequate to the task of raising their own children.

Damned if You Do ...

I once asked a psychologist about feelings of frustration and difficulty holding on to one's temper. "Is this about people in general, or about you?" he asked, and I admitted I was concerned about the way Josh's AS wore me down. "You're an Asperger parent," the psychologist said. "You'd be crazy if you *didn't* feel that way." I'm paraphrasing; he might not have actually used the word "crazy." But the message was clear.

That certainly doesn't excuse unreasonable behavior on the part of parents. This is not a "get-out-of-jail-free" card for child abusers; those who hurt their children are either mentally ill people or criminals, and should be treated as such. But we have to understand that all parents encounter frustration, and parents of children with Asperger Syndrome are likely to encounter more than most. We're not always going to be perfect. We're not always going to react the way we wish we could. We're not always going to be Dr. Huxtable, dealing with his children with a chuckle on a rerun of *The Cosby Show*.

This feeling is exacerbated by the fact that our children don't always show outward signs of a medical condition. So society will judge our parenting skills by their behavior, which is often outside the norm. And our behavior, which is heightened by the feeling that all eyes are upon us, is not always exemplary.

It's important to examine *why* we're even concerned about the opinion of those we pass in the street or meet at the mall. If we know we're doing the right thing for our children, we should stand tall and do it. What strangers may believe should be irrelevant.

Unfortunately, many of us – especially when we're new to the autism spectrum – *do* care what everyone else thinks. We may still be struggling with issues that we have some fault, some failing that caused this problem for our children. And we have to realize that most of the judgment, most of the disapproval, we feel is not coming from outside; it's coming from us.

"That's an individual issue for parents, about how much power we want to give to other people to control how we feel about ourselves," says Jed E. Baker, Ph.D., a New Jersey psychologist whose practice includes many AS social skills groups. "That's the way I would put it to a parent. How much power are you going to give to somebody who has little understanding? They haven't walked a mile in your shoes. How much are you going to care and really give power to this person to control your life, which they don't have to lead?"

Sometimes, just getting out of bed in the morning is a victory.

The Look

Just as bad as the feeling that people think you're a monster are the accusatory looks of other parents who think you're not doing *enough* to control your child's behavior. When a hungry, cranky child at the local Burger King starts to whine about the milk being warm, parents nod their heads in recognition and empathy. When a hungry, cranky child with Asperger Syndrome has a four-alarm meltdown because the milk is warm, and we try calmly to placate him, we get The Look. When we try to reason with our children, try to work around the immediate problem by accommodating their strict adherence to routine or their sensitivity to sound, touch, or taste, we get The Look.

The Look is that easily recognizable expression that says, "Hey, be an adult. Don't let a child run your life. If you *knew about discipline*, there wouldn't be a problem." The Look is the signal that the adult you're dealing with hasn't heard of, or doesn't understand, AS.

That is key to your sanity: you have to remember that this person *hasn't heard of or doesn't understand AS*. Is it wrong for someone else to judge your parenting skills based on one incident? Of course it is. Is it wrong that they're going to judge you at all? Of course it is. Is it natural that this will happen? Of course it is.

We live in a society that judges, whether we like to admit it or not. We see television reports about people accused of crimes, and we decide on the merits of a two-minute news story whether we think they're guilty or not. We watch the Academy Awards on TV and judge which celebrities are "real people" and which ones are "stuck up" based on what they're wearing. We make assumptions about people based on how they decorate their homes, what kind of car they drive, which political candidate they endorse with a bumper sticker and what we see them buying at the supermarket. If we see someone wearing the cap of a team we root against, we tend to think of them as the opposition. If we hear music we like coming from the stereo in the car next to us at the red light, we believe we have found a kindred spirit.

Judgments are made in a flash, and they can be based on anything. And when something very noticeable, like an Asperger Syndrome tantrum, occurs in public, we are not only dealing with the immediate situation, we're dealing with the *perception* of the situation, and the *impression* it's making on the people who can observe it.

Our choices are clear: we can decide not to care about the impressions we give people who are uninformed or misinformed. That's probably the healthiest choice, and the one that will be made least often. We can try to educate the world about AS and the ways in which it manifests itself, so the world can better understand and judge less harshly. That's most likely the best overall choice, but it requires years of education and tireless effort on the part of people who are, almost to a person, not us. Another choice is to let all the attention bother us and try to explain to everyone present at the time that this is a neurological condition and you're neither coddling nor manhandling your child. Good luck with that one.

Education, though, is key. Maybe you can't explain AS to the other shoppers at Target while the incident is going on, but getting the word out can't do anything but help. Press coverage on ABC News and in *The New York Times* began with parents who wanted AS to be seen, and understood, by people across the country. Lori Shery, the founder and president of ASPEN, says her group's function, beyond supporting parents of children with AS, is to educate.

"You really become your child's advocate. I think it's all part of the coping process," she says. "That's one of my main roles, to educate the public. So there'll be more understanding. Even if they're not going to be empathetic or sympathetic, at least they won't be judgmental."

Clearly, the best choice is to try to prepare for public incidents (and by "public," we can mean any time anyone except immediate family is present), so we can either avoid them entirely, or have a plan to deal with them in as unobtrusive a fashion as possible.

The first step is to forgive yourself for not being perfect. It's hard to do, but very important. Keep in mind that you're going to make mistakes, that your emotions will occasionally override your intellect, and that you're up against an obstacle nine out of ten parents will never have to face. Expecting to react in the proper manner every single time isn't just unrealistic, it's destructive. Because you *won't* react properly to every stimulus, and when you don't, you'll feel guilty about it. That doesn't help anything.

Asperger Syndrome doesn't give you much of a break, either. I remember one evening when Josh was about seven, and he was doing his level best to get a reaction out of me. I was in a mellow mood that night, letting things slide off my back, so he was having little success, and that bothered him. He kept at it, and at it, and at it. AS doesn't allow for much in the way of adaptability. He had set his mind to this task, and he'd see it through to the end.

When I was putting him to bed that night, telling him to have a good night and that I'd see him in the morning, he started poking me in the chest with one finger. I'd talk, and he'd poke. His eyes narrowed; he still wasn't getting the reaction he wanted. Finally, my patience about worn out, I blurted out, "What are you *doing*?"

"I'm pushing your buttons," my seven-year-old son replied.

There is no escape. Because AS isn't as "obvious" a condition as other disabilities, we sometimes fall into the trap of forgetting that our children won't always react to things the way other kids do. If they're doing well at school, are conversant at home, getting their homework done and not throwing tantrums, we are lulled into complacency. But that can be dangerous, because eventually the wear and tear of living with an individual with AS will take its toll, and if we're not ready, we'll react badly.

So preparation is vital. Notice the behaviors that, whether your child intends them to or not, especially irritate your sensibilities. It's best to make note of them during a normal day, in the privacy of your home, and file the information away in your head. Think about what kind of reaction you want to have when that behavior surfaces the next time. Spend time consciously deciding on a reaction and if you have to, rehearse it.

The reaction doesn't have to be a specific action; it can be an attitude. It can be emulating someone who handles the same kind of situation better than you do. I've often practiced reacting to Josh the way my wife does, explaining to him, asking him questions in an even tone, because she has more patience than I do. When I've been able to remember that trick, it has worked very well. The problem is remembering.

The moment of truth comes when your child pushes that particular hot button again. Because it's predisposed toward eliciting an emotional reaction from you specifically, it's hard to take that moment and remember your carefully prepared reaction.

It can be something as simple as counting to three before you say anything. It can be the idea of taking a deep breath. *Anything* that gives you a moment to think, to react other than emotionally, is the key. Once you have that in place, you can handle most situations your child's AS will throw at you.

The key in that last sentence is the word "most." It isn't the word "all." And that's by design. Nobody can handle every situation the right way; some can't even react properly half the time. But any improvement over a bad situation is worth making. That doesn't mean you're going to be perfect, and it doesn't mean you'll be horrible. You'll be human, which means sometimes you'll make mistakes and sometimes you'll do well.

There is no shame in making a mistake. It's making the *same* mistake over and over again that's the problem.

You have to recognize patterns in your own behavior, as well as your child's. Which behaviors do you react to most strongly? Are food issues more irritating to you than stimming? Why? Which scenarios does your spouse find especially maddening, but you don't? Analyze that. Is there a time of the day when you're testier than usual, but perhaps your spouse is more mellow? Maybe it's best, when both of you are present, to divide the parental duty that way: if a situation arises that really gets your goat, call your spouse. If your child is exhibiting a behavior that is guaranteed to get a rise out of your spouse, but not you, step in when you can. Calmer heads are always better. And, as we'll discuss later on, single parents generally have it twice as hard as those who work in pairs. Their solutions will, by definition, have to be different.

Forgiveness

Understand it now: there will be times when you won't react the way you want to. It's not a good thing, but it's a true one. There are two keys to dealing with it: first, never let anything get completely out of hand; and second, think it over afterward, and forgive yourself.

A mother of an eleven-year-old boy I know told me about a time her son was clearly trying to get her angry, and did so expertly. The boy knew exactly which behaviors would make his mother react and, for some reason, one night he thought that would be a fine form of entertainment. He started calling her names. Once a child with AS decides to call you names, he has two courses of action: come up with every possible synonym for the irritating name he started with, or use the same one over and over for hours at a time.

In this case, the boy used the second option, calling his mother a name (it doesn't matter which one), no matter what she said to him or how she reacted. She was home alone with the boy that night, and tried every possible tactic – ignoring the child, explaining that what he was doing was rude and annoying, threatening punishment, then actually employing the punishment, which was loss of TV for the night.

The boy was addicted to a certain show broadcast on that night, so he reacted vehemently. He cursed at his mother, refused to move from the sofa, grabbed the remote control and turned the television back on every time she turned it off. In the meantime, he screamed and cried and continued to call her the name.

Finally, she reached the end of her rope. She slapped her son in the face. Not hard enough to hurt him, but enough to get his attention, and he started to cry. It was a very bad night.

After the crying (on both ends) was over, the mother had some choices to make. First, she took some minutes to think about what had happened, and to calm her emotions. Then she went to her son's room, apologized for hitting him, explained again why she had been so angry, and hugged him. He told her he didn't know why he'd been trying to get her angry, but acknowledged that was exactly what he was trying to do.

They had a very good conversation after that, and the storm passed. But for the mother, the hard part was forgiving herself for raising a hand to her son.

"I couldn't believe I'd done it," she said. "I had felt like it before, you know, because sometimes I get so angry. But I'd always managed to stop myself before I did anything like that."

She spent a few days in a funk, thinking she was an awful parent and wondering if the situation would ever arise again, and how she would react. It wasn't until she realized her son was behaving normally, for him, and seemed to have put the incident behind him, that she could do the same herself.

"It wasn't that I thought, 'well, he's forgotten about it, so I can forget about it,'" she said. "But I figured that maybe if he could let me off the hook for the one time I didn't do what I should, maybe I could, too."

She also chose to focus on the many times she had wanted to react that way, and had stopped herself. "I thought back, and there had been a lot of times when I'd been almost that angry," she said. "My husband said to me later that I'd handled ninety-nine out of a hundred situations right. And I hadn't hurt (our son) at all, even the time I didn't handle it right."

My friend now says she and her son have a stronger relationship, not because of the incident, but because of the way they handled the aftermath of the incident. It's not a bad lesson to learn.

The Look, Part 2

One of the problems with The Look is the way it makes you feel about yourself. The other is the way it makes you feel about your child.

Because – no matter how much we deny it – we do care what other people think about us, The Look can be devastating. It can make us feel like inadequate parents. It can make us see our children through the eyes of the world outside the AS community, and that can be a devastating, saddening experience.

"You see that society is rejecting them, rejects them all long, and we have to constantly face that," says Sharon Graebener, mother of ten-year-old Max. "There's always that (feeling that society is saying), 'there's something wrong with you, you're no good, you shouldn't be here.' I just feel that and you have to say, 'no, you're wrong.' Sometimes I have a hard time with that."

When I was growing up, there was a boy in my class whom we'll call Herbert. Herbert was "the weird kid." He didn't look the rest of us in the eye. He didn't talk like the rest of us. He always had some weird piece of information he wanted to talk about, and didn't want to hear about the things the rest of us kids were discussing. He didn't have a favorite Beatle (this was in the sixties, after all). I'm not sure he even knew about the Beatles.

Naturally, Herbert was the butt of many jokes, the loser of many a schoolyard fistfight, and the object of great ridicule in our class. In retrospect, I have to believe Herbert was a child with AS, or a similar condition. And since I was among those who made fun of him and treated him so badly, I feel especially sorry about it. Because now I'm raising a Herbert of my own.

I know what many people see when they look at my son. And while I know they're wrong, I can understand the conclusions to which they often jump. I want to explain to them all that they don't really understand, that this is the kind of child he is and that eventually he'll learn to use his differences to his advantage, that there isn't a kinder soul on this planet, but of course I can't do that. And when I see The Look in their eyes that there must have been in mine when I was a boy on the playground with Herbert, it is devastating.

What I have to remember about The Look is that it's an uninformed Look. It says, "I don't really understand the situation, but I'm going to pass judgment on it anyway." It's a natural reaction, but an erroneous one. And Joshua is without question not to blame for it. He is, in some ways, more mature than his father. Because he accepts himself for what he is and doesn't worry about the way the world sees him.

It's one way in which his AS works to his advantage. In not taking note of a world outside his own head, he spares himself the hurt that world will send his way. In not caring that someone might see him behaving outside the accepted "norm," he allows himself to truly be himself more than the rest of us, who behave the way we think we're supposed to behave, can manage.

The Look isn't going to go away. But we don't have to let it change the way we raise our children.

Why I Tell Everyone About AS

*I*UNDERSTAND THE PARENTS WHO DON'T want to talk about their children's Asperger Syndrome. I've seen the pitying looks other adults give. I've heard the ridiculous questions ("can my child catch it from him?"). And I know what it feels like to have to repeat the same explanation time after time after time. Some things aren't other people's business, and it can feel like your child's AS is one of them.

Still, on a Sunday morning in July of 1999, I told 34 million strangers about my son's AS. It was not a decision made lightly, and I'm still not sure it was the best one, but it certainly had its upside.

I wrote about Josh in the July 18, 1999 edition of *USA Weekend*, the newspaper insert that reaches 34 million homes every weekend. It was an assignment that a freelance writer like myself cherishes, since it is seen in an enormous number of

21

households and raises the profile of the subject and the writer, something that can never be bad for business.

But I hadn't planned on talking about Josh in the article; I had pitched it to the magazine as a general story on AS. I thought the 2.5 million or so people with the condition would make it a universal enough subject, but the editors had another idea.

"Let's make it more personal," one suggested to me. "We'd really be interested if you could write about your son and your own experience."

This was a relatively blatant ploy. The editors at *USA Weekend* wanted me to write what I call a "smiling-through-the-pain" story about AS, about how awful it is to be the parent of an "afflicted" child and how we, as a family, are "fighting this disease." It's not at all unusual, and not a bad way to market such an article. It just wasn't what I'd had in mind. I didn't mean to ask millions for pity; I didn't need it, and neither did Josh. And the idea that millions of strangers would be waking up to read about my son and his hand-flapping, commercial-singing, social-skills-deficient condition was not a cause for celebration in my house.

There were considerations. First, would Josh have to be identified by name? Yes, he would. But we could certainly leave out of the article the name of the town we live in, and any information that might compromise his safety. That was not negotiable. Josh wasn't even ten years old yet.

Then, my wife and I had a long talk about the implications. It was one thing, we agreed, to tell friends, relatives and neighbors about Josh's AS, but millions of people all over the country? Even in our community, kids in his school could misunderstand. Josh's tantrums could be scary; we'd known parents who didn't want their children playing with our daughter because Josh would be in the house. Multiply that geometrically, and the problems could be more than we could handle.

Finally, I talked to Josh about it. At first, he listened very carefully to my explanation that this would be an article about people like him, and that it would discuss how they were differ-ent from most of us. It would explain these differences, and try to help people understand why people like him were people like him.

"I'm not *that* different," he said.

"No, you're not," I agreed. "But sometimes you do things, or you act in a way, that people don't understand." He knew I meant his stimming, his reluctance to make eye contact, and other symptoms we had discussed before.

"Will bullies see it?" he wanted to know. At that time, Josh was the target of some schoolyard toughs who wanted to see how easily he could be made to lose his temper.

"They might," I admitted. "I can't guarantee that people in your school won't read the article."

"I don't want you to do it," Josh said.

"I don't blame you," I answered. "But I want you to think about it. Because there may be some people out there whose kids have Asperger Syndrome and who don't know about it. And if they read the article, they could find out what their kids' problems are, and maybe get them the kind of help you've been getting."

He walked away and thought about that for a few minutes, then came back to my desk, where I was working. "Let's go ahead and write the story," Josh said. "If I can help other people like me, I should do it." I've rarely been more proud of him.

I wrote the article in November 1998. Because it was what the publishers call "an evergreen," meaning it wasn't tied to some specific event, the story could run in the supplement on any given Sunday. It was months before I heard from the editors again.

When I did, they wanted pictures to go with the article. Pictures of me and Josh. I balked. No pictures of Josh's face, I insisted. There are too many dangerous strangers out there when your kid's face *isn't* showing up on 34 million doorsteps. The edi-tors agreed. But they wanted pictures of Josh, taken from behind, with his face obscured.

The photographer showed up after school one day, taking pictures of Josh and me in front of our home. Josh loved it; he thought it was very funny that I kept moving his face away from the camera every time the man wanted to take a picture. At one point, he was laughing so hard, he buried his head in my chest. The photographer snapped the shutter. The picture that showed up on America's front step was one that looked exactly as if my son were crying into my chest as I held him, trying to soothe his tears. Actually, he was laughing too hard to control himself, but *USA Weekend* got its "smiling-through-the-pain" shot.

On July 18, 1999, the article hit the streets, and immediately, our phone began to ring. Our neighbors across the street, whose daughter is a close friend of our daughter, called to say they "understand Josh a little better now." I should point out that these people were never among those who kept their child away from our daughter because of Josh, but welcomed Josh into their home on a regular basis and never blinked an eye. But their understanding was important.

Lori Shery, the president of ASPEN, called a few times that weekend, and emailed more often. She said the ASPEN web site, which I had mentioned in the article, usually got about fifty "hits" a day at that time (it has since increased enormously), but in the two weeks after the article ran, over nineteen thousand were recorded. And Lori received 1,000 emails through the ASPEN site.

A few of the emails were reason enough to have written the article. "It's fantastic that the word is getting out ... please pass on a great big 'thank you' to Jeffrey Cohen from me," read one. Another – my favorite – said, "Lori: Just read (actually, reread) your forwarding of Jeff Cohen's incredible article. I wanted to say I was as moved this time as I was the first time I read it. The difference is that this time, as I read, I smiled slightly, knowingly. The first time I read it, I had ice-cold chills running up and down my spine and goosebumps all over – this man was talking about my son! IN EVERY WAY! Thanks to Jeff's article, we finally had a name/word/condition/SOMETHING to grab onto in the dizzying world that described our life with our AS son. Through Jeff's article I got in touch with you and ASPEN, I've been to conferences, support meetings, spent lots of time on the web ... but MOST MOST MOST importantly and important to me, I am so much better able to understand my son, and he is SO SO SO much better off for it. If you're a friend of Jeff's, please tell him he has my heartfelt thanks."

You're welcome.

"Going Public"

Deciding to "go public" with your child's AS is a decision you make for your child and for yourself. It certainly doesn't have to be on so grand a scale. Going public can be as simple as admitting to yourself that there's a problem and having it diagnosed. It can be a matter of explaining the condition to your family, to your friends and to the school system your child attends.

In our case, we decided to tell people about Josh's AS because when he was diagnosed in 1995, almost no one had heard of Asperger Syndrome. It was as much a matter of educating the people he'd need for help as it was a decision not to be bashful. But for you, it could be a more difficult, more distasteful decision. It's a matter of personal taste and emotion. Some things are inherently more difficult for some people to "share" than others, and I can't tell you what kind of person you are. People *will* talk, and if that's going to bother you to the point of distraction, you had better consider it before you "go public."

What it comes down to is this: tell the people you want to tell. Tell them as much as you want to tell them. But don't be ashamed, because AS is nothing to be embarrassed about.

It's one thing to know that intellectually. It's quite another to understand it emotionally.

Some parents are mortified when their children exhibit symptoms in public. Especially for children with AS, who have difficulty "fitting in" and being accepted by their peers, it's painful to be publicly "different." Parents, who have a broader perspective than their children with AS, see every incident as a setback. They feel that their children are that much further from making friends, being accepted, and being happy.

The children with AS, because they don't pick up social signals easily, aren't at all concerned about their behavior in public, or anywhere else. It's the parents who are embarrassed, and the parents who try to rein in the behavior, to have their children seem more "normal." It's an understandable impulse.

And it works for some parents. Eventually, with great patience and hours of practice, the child learns not to exhibit that particular behavior when other people are present. My wife and I spent years trying to get Josh to stop flapping his arms when he became excited. We tried to get him to limit that behavior to his room, where we told him he can do whatever makes him feel good. But the best we could do was to condense the behavior, make it smaller. Josh doesn't flap his arms anymore, but he does raise his fingers to his face and waggle them. It's the same reaction, but he's made the action smaller. That's Josh's way of dealing with it.

Another child with AS I know, who is eleven years old, would run up to other children (and some adults) and poke them by way of greeting. This became so routine to those who knew him that they barely noticed, but each year his new classmates would find it very off-putting, and some parents complained to the school. The boy's mother spoke with his teachers at the beginning of every school year and tried to explain his behavior to other parents, but the school found it difficult to deal with. Anything involving touching is always a problem.

Once a week the boy, whom we'll call Jared, was going to a social skills group run by a psychologist outside the school. The other boys in his group, and the professional who ran it, knew Jared wasn't trying to hurt anyone with his poking; that it was just his way of greeting. The psychologist suggested to Jared's mother that they begin the school year by talking directly to his class, introducing them to Jared and explaining AS so the other kids would know Jared wasn't trying to hurt or annoy them; he was just saying hello.

A lot of parents face this choice. Should they make an open statement in the classroom about the child with AS? In some cases, it can create as many problems as it solves. If the children in the class are given to teasing, or if the child with AS is especially sensitive about his "differences," making a presentation to the class can be exactly the wrong thing to do. It can end up increasing the child's sense of embarrassment, and underlining the idea that he's not the same as the rest of the students in the class.

Jared's mother decided to go ahead with a talk to the class, and arranged for the psychologist to come to the school during the first week of the new term to explain Jared's behavior. Jared was given the option of leaving the room while the talk was going on, but he chose to stay. Afterward the kids in his class understood him a little better. He went on to have a banner year. Since then, his mother has made it a point to perform what she calls "the dog and pony show" every September when school starts again.

That's just one case; it would have been just as easy, and perhaps just as successful, to decide not to make a point of the student's AS. You know your child, and the school system, better than anyone else, and you have to "go with your gut."

The problems come with parents who are embarrassed that their children aren't perfect. My wife and I decided to become what she calls "the AS poster children" because we thought it was important to get the word out that Asperger Syndrome is *not* something to be embarrassed about. You don't have to go that far (and there are times I still wonder if we've gone too far; Josh didn't sign on to be the spokesman for AS – he's just living his life), but to try and hide the condition is to send your child the implied message that there's something wrong with him so shameful it's best not to talk about it. And that can't ever be a good thing.

So it comes down to a question of degree. How much do you talk about AS, and how often? Do you tell people when they ask, or volunteer the information? Do what you're comfortable doing, but remember that AS is not a flaw, and it's not a shame. It's just a facet of your child. And it always will be.

Keep in mind, too, that educating "the public" is a way to diminish whatever stigma you may see about your child's AS. The more people who know, and understand, the condition, the easier it will be to explain. And the fewer "cringe-moments" there will be. No one need be ashamed of Asperger Syndrome, and once the world knows that, no one will be.

Millennium Dreamer

By the way, there's a postscript to the *USA Weekend* saga. In fact, *two* postscripts.

First, the article was published in July, when school was out of session. It wasn't planned that way; the story had been written eight months before, but wasn't published until there was an appropriate spot for it in the magazine. The timing turned out to be an advantage, however, because Josh didn't have to deal with the kids he called "the bullies," the ones who would have made fun of him and waited for his temper, which is formidable, to kick in.

When school started in September, there were a couple of comments within Josh's earshot. One boy told Josh he'd read in the newspaper that Josh had "a disease," and the boy figured he shouldn't play with Josh for fear of catching it. Josh got a little upset, but the paraprofessional who works with him said he handled it well.

I asked him about it when he got home from school that day. Josh, who is more introspective than he lets on, took a moment to think about it, then said, "If he'd really read the article, he'd know he can't catch it from me." Then, without warning, he added, "Sometimes I like having Asperger Syndrome."

"Really?" I asked. We've never told him he *shouldn't* like it, but that took me by surprise.

"Yeah. It helps my imagination." Sometimes, Joshua's AS helps him put things in perspective. It gave me new reason to be proud of my son.

The second postscript was considerably more spectacular. After the teasing he took when he went back to school, I decided Josh deserved a reward for letting his story be told to so many people he'd never met. But, since the fee I'd gotten from *USA Weekend* had been spent on trifles like shelter and food, I was looking for the best way to repay him for his selflessness without taking out a home equity loan to pay for it.

One night surfing the Internet, it found me. The Walt Disney Company and McDonald's were sponsoring a program called "Millennium Dreamers" (this was just before the beginning of the year 2000), honoring young people who had done something to help their communities or people other than themselves. An adult had to nominate the child, explain why he or she deserved the honor, and various forms needed to be filled out. The child had to write a short essay. Another adult, not a parent, had to sign forms and write a paragraph on why the child should be a Millennium Dreamer.

It sounded like a perfect solution, except I was sure we didn't have a chance to be included. Still, it seemed worth the effort to try. After all the hurdles were jumped, the forms were sent in, and we forgot about it. But in February of 2000, a package arrived from Disney saying Josh had been selected, as one of 2,000 kids, for a four-day stay at Walt Disney World in Florida, courtesy of Disney and McDonald's.

That May, Joshua and his family (that is, myself, my wife, and Eve) spent four days as guests in a huge theme park, treated as well as two huge corporations can treat people when they put their minds to it. Some of the other Millennium Dreamers had overcome diseases and helped others who suffered from the same afflictions. Others had organized programs to preserve the environment, or to help people in their communities who had fallen on hard times. Each had a story to tell, and there were many members of the press waiting to hear them.

Josh, however, didn't want to answer any questions about why he was there. He seemed a little shy about it, and it wasn't until the last night, when the festivities were being brought to a close, that he told me why he'd asked not to talk to the reporters.

"I didn't want them to ask me why I was here," he said, "because I don't really understand why I'm here. I didn't do anything. You wrote the article."

"Yes," I told him, "but I wouldn't have written it if you hadn't agreed to it. And you only did that because you knew it would help other people."

Josh shook his head. He hadn't done anything. And that is my son: he's not embarrassed about having Asperger Syndrome, but he isn't crazy about people fawning over him when he does something for others. He doesn't see it as a big deal.

"Going public" might not have been such a bad idea, after all.

The Debate Over Inclusion

$\mathcal{L}$ET'S GET ONE THING STRAIGHT right from the start – I'm not going to tell you whether your child should be in a special education program, a self-contained classroom, a private school, be home schooled or included in what used to be called mainstream classes. Not only am I absolutely unqualified to do so, but even a licensed expert on the subject couldn't make such a recommendation without knowing the child in question well. Every child is different.

Besides, remember: this book is *not* about your child. It's about you. But the inclusion debate, which has raged for some years in the special education community, will touch on you at some point, if it hasn't already. You'll have to make a decision, and you'll have to live with the decision you make. A little information on the debate wouldn't be an awful thing.

With my son, there was never much debate. He did attend a special pre-kindergarten in our school district briefly, but we were advised by the program staff to remove him from the class because they didn't "see any problem." That was in 1994, and the term "Asperger Syndrome" hadn't been heard in our district yet. Things have changed since then. Now, everybody in any school in our town knows Joshua's name, and knows there are a number of other children diagnosed with AS in the district.

Once Josh started kindergarten, the teacher *did* notice a problem, and we began talking to members of the school district's child study team, which took a family history, observed him in the classroom, consulted with therapists and actually paid for us to have Josh examined by a pediatric neurologist, all of which led up to his diagnosis.

While we were still searching for a name to assign to whatever was making Josh act the way he did, my wife attended a conference given by a group not far from where we live, focusing on a growing diagnosis in the autism spectrum: Asperger Syndrome. She listened to the speaker, becoming more convinced with each passing minute that this was exactly Josh's condition.

And on the way out for the lunch break, she ran into our school district's psychologist and speech therapist, who looked her in the eye and said, "a-*ha*!"

Your school system may not be as cooperative as the one where I live. I've heard stories of some districts that are downright hostile, and it can even vary from school to school and teacher to teacher. Some school districts prefer to "ship out" children with AS, pay to send them to private schools for children with autism spectrum disorders. A friend of Josh's travels on a bus for close to an hour each way every day because his district prefers not to take on the challenge his AS presents. Ironically, he is bused to a private school in the town where my family lives. If Josh's friend lived here, he probably wouldn't be in that school; he'd be in the public school system right here in town.

We were never advised to remove Josh from his usual class, or to use the resource room in the school he attended; it wasn't necessary. He did attend the school district's transitional primary program between kindergarten and first grade for a year, and it helped enormously in teaching him what was expected of him, and in giving him the time he needed to mature a little and get ready for the school experience that was ahead of him.

Also, since second grade, Josh has had the help of a para-professional, Joyce Gregus, who was assigned to him by the child study team. Joyce keeps in close contact with my wife and me, and she stays in class with Josh all day, "hanging back" most of the time, but jumping in when Josh needs help in a social situation or in just getting through the challenges of what for other kids would be a normal day.

Other parents have had different experiences. Depending on the school system, I've heard tales of children with AS being isolated in hallways during a tantrum, being labeled "behavior problems" and sent home on a regular basis. I've heard that some districts actually recommend home schooling for children with autism spectrum disorders, whether that is feasible for the parents in question or not.

Some school systems have a special affinity for "self-contained classrooms," which keep children in the public school, but generally isolated from the rest of the school population. This is seen as a "middle ground" between complete inclusion and isolation, and is sometimes used for only certain periods of the day. But the debate about self-contained classrooms, special schools and inclusion goes on.

It's Not You

The first thing to keep in mind when you're faced with a hostile school official or school district is that it's not your fault (unless you've initiated the hostility, but we'll get to that in a later chapter). It's not your child's fault, either. In fact, it doesn't matter whose fault it is. What matters is how you're going to deal with the situation.

Parents run the gamut. Some have secretly always wanted to home school their children, and immediately offer that as an option. Others, in cases where both parents have to work outside the home, are very happy with private schools whose staffs are especially trained to deal with children on the autism spectrum. And, in some cases, municipal school districts will pay the (often exorbitant) tuition for private schools, because they feel they can't handle the behavior of the child with AS under normal circumstances.

Self-contained classrooms and resource rooms have lost some of their popularity over the past few years. Again, there are parents on both sides of the issue: some feel that any contact with neurotypical peers is a benefit, while others feel that self-contained classrooms stigmatize the students, and leave them open to teasing and abuse from their peers in school.

I'm not here to tell you if any of these options is for you. I'm here to tell you to fight for the one you choose, or to fight for the school district to keep your child in a general education class, if that is what you decide.

How *do* you decide? No one knows your child better than you and your spouse or family. You probably already have some instincts on what would be best. But you have to fight against the impulse to take care of the problem in the easiest, most conciliatory way available, possibly ignoring what's best for your child. That's not as easy as it sounds.

If you're like me (and hopefully you're not, in this respect), you cringe at the thought that someone might be upset with you. And the idea of walking into a principal's office (or a school superintendent's, or some other administrator's) still worries many of us who tried to obey the rules when we were in school. Marry those two thoughts together, and you have a reaction you feel very strongly and probably can't explain: fear.

I have seen adults with advanced degrees blanch at the thought of making trouble in the school system. But keep this in mind: you're *not* making trouble; you're advocating for your child. And your child needs your help considerably more than you need to be liked by everyone in the school system.

Also, dealing with AS on a daily basis is a grueling, tiring experience. Battling an autism spectrum condition can be more exhausting on a day-to-day basis than most things I can imagine. There is no let-up; there is no "time off," unless you go far out of your way to create it. Sometimes, if someone from a school district – a psychologist, social worker, teacher or administrator – suggests that your child would be better off in a school "better suited to his needs," it's awfully tempting to take that route. That would mean no more battles with the district, and fewer days spent getting gray hairs over a possible "incident" when you should be working.

And I can't stress this enough – for some families, this is the right choice to make. Some children thrive in private schools, some do wonderfully well with home schooling. Inclusion isn't the only alternative, and for some people, it's not even the best alternative. But if you decide that it is the best fit for your child, you can't back down, and you can't give in to the desire to make things "nice and easy" for yourself or the schools. You have to gear yourself up for a series of tooth and nail dogfights that may last until your child is ensconced in the college or career of his or her choice.

Lori Shery of ASPEN says her son Adam has been included throughout his school career (he is now a high school student). She talks to parents who are deciding about school placement all the time. "I think in a perfect world, the best placement for a school-age child is in a regular classroom in a public school with supports that are needed," she says. "However, there are districts that either don't get it or don't want to get it. They don't want to make the effort for the child. Yes, the parents could take them to court, and then the district would have to do it, but that wouldn't be a very positive environment for the child to be in. In those cases, private special schools may be better placements. I'm not a fan of self-contained classes, because they isolate the children."

My wife and I decided to push for inclusion, and we were lucky to live in a cooperative school district that believes in it more than almost any other I've ever seen. But we do not send Josh to a "mainstream" summer camp. He attends a day camp during the summer that is specifically intended for children with autism spectrum disorders, with ADD and ADHD, and other neurological conditions. A number of factors led to this decision.

First, there was the fact that we enrolled him in a "regular" camp one summer, and although there were one or two incidents that we were informed about where Josh had lost his temper and behaved inappropriately, overall he seemed to have a good time without much fuss. Anyway, that was what we thought, until I called in late September to re-enroll Josh for the following year, and was told the camp "couldn't accommodate him next year." It was like being kicked out of nursery school all over again.

Also, after a ten-month school year, Josh needed to let off a little steam. He'd been holding it together the best he could from September to June, and adding social stress to his days during the summer wasn't worth the emotional toll it would take on him, and on us. We needed a camp that employed specially trained counselors, one where the other children had their own behaviors to deal with and were more likely to leave Josh alone. In short, we needed a place where he could be with other kids who were like him. We found such a place, luckily, when we attended a camp fair out of desperation as summer was rapidly approaching.

It was a relief I can't adequately describe. A social skills specialist was on hand every day to mediate disagreements. The staff was trained, and recognized AS for what it is, so they were able to work with Josh without the extreme reaction the "uninitiated" sometimes offer. He made friends and kept them. And he didn't come home stressed out at the end of the day.

So why not extend that situation to the school year and send Josh to a private program geared toward students with autism spectrum disorders? Because to us, summer is a time dedicated to enjoyment, and the rest of the year, you deal with the real world. Josh has made enormous progress in his "real-world" school, and we wouldn't want to interrupt that. But for ten weeks during the summer, it's okay to relax and just be Josh.

It's Not Them, Either

When someone says your child shouldn't be taught in a public school's inclusive class, the first impulse is to assume the school system is looking for the easy way out. They don't *want* to work with your child, so they're sending him off to another place and washing their hands of the "problem."

There's no doubt that this is the case in some instances, but it usually is not. Schools don't exist to *not* teach children, and teachers don't go through college and graduate school in order to avoid anyone who doesn't fit the typical mold.

However, in many districts, even those that promote the idea of inclusion, the paraprofessionals and teachers on staff are not sufficiently trained to deal with less obvious issues like those presented by Asperger Syndrome.

"I do sympathize with teachers who basically get children dumped on them, who have no training or support or resources," says Lori Shery. She cites New Jersey state law, which says, "'each district board of education shall have policies, procedures and programs in effect to ensure … the in-service training needs for professional and paraprofessional staff who provide special education, general education or related services, are identified, and that appropriate in-service training is provided.' It's the words 'appropriate' and 'needs.' That's where we have the problem," Lori says.

Laws on the subject vary from state to state, and some school districts are more open to inclusion than others. If your child hasn't started school yet, it's a good idea to get a feel for the district, and based on your decision to keep your child in an inclusive class or not, prepare to make your case at a meeting. In most cases, a child study team will be called upon to observe your child, make recommendations and meet with you about your child's case.

"The child's behavioral ability, any particular academic learning needs, all these are taken into consideration," says John Masters, director of educational services for the school district of Highland Park, New Jersey. He says the state has mandated that inclusion be the first priority for all children considered disabled in any way. "By New Jersey state law, we're obligated to consider the general education class first. You start out with the consideration that every child has the right to be in a general education program."

If it is determined that the child can't participate in a general education program without help, the next step is to determine what help is necessary, and if possible, to provide it, he says. "If the child is having difficulties, (it must be determined) what kind of things you can do to accommodate the child's needs to (help him) be in that general education program," Masters says. "Only when the child's needs can't be met in a general education class do you start looking at other kinds of programs outside of the classroom. But you're obligated to try within reason things that would benefit the child being there."

But Dennis Debbaudt, a licensed private investigator and writer on the subject of the criminal justice system as it pertains to the autism spectrum, is not a strong believer in inclusion.

"Without a healthy and strong and effective public awareness campaign, (which would begin) before a student starts attending school, not after, our kids are at risk in these inclusionary programs," says Debbaudt, who works with families whose children on the autism spectrum have gotten into trouble with the law. "I know that's not very popular. The fact is, most of the cases I'm hearing about are kids who are in inclusionary programs in school. They don't know how to handle it, and nobody knows they're on the spectrum. (Parents and the school districts) don't want to go into the school and do an effective public awareness campaign for everybody in that school, from the principal to the janitor, the parents of the other kids, the other students, all the teachers, everybody. They don't want to do that, and they're not doing that."

Even within school districts – and within schools – the level of tolerance for "different" students can vary, though. "You can have a different situation among different schools within a school district, or classroom to classroom," John Masters admits. "Different teachers have different tolerance levels, and then you have to work with those teachers who are less tolerant. It's the child's right to be there, and our obligation to protect that right."

The child study team, the administration, the classroom teacher (or teachers) and the parents should all be part of the decision-making process. Masters says some parents would be happier to see their children in special education classes, or otherwise not included in general classes.

"The hardest part of this whole thing is that sometimes the general education class is not the place to best address the child's needs," Masters says. "If you're teaching reading so differently than the way it's being taught in the classroom, you can't do it in the same place. Whether it's a skill thing, or because it would embarrass the child, it's not the thing to do. The only other circumstance is when the child's behavior is so disruptive that it interferes with the other children's rights to get an education."

Some parents are not pleased when their children can't be included in general classes, while others feel inclusion is absolutely the wrong program for their children. Not speaking about AS parents in particular, Masters says, "In some cases, parents don't see inclusion as the way to meet their children's needs. I don't think it has to be all or nothing. I believe in the least restrictive environment. When we are moving a child to a separate setting, it really is special education, because we're doing something very special for that child that we don't do anywhere else. But the ultimate goal always is to meet the child's needs so that child can eventually be included in general education again."

Many parents of children with AS report experiences that don't seem to be as accommodating and inclusion-minded as what Masters describes, but some states require more stringent inclusion programs than New Jersey, although "everybody is pretty much in the same boat." Still, it's impossible to be an AS parent without having experienced, or at least heard, a horror story or two.

One mother, who asked me not to mention her name or the school district, says her nine-year-old son's teacher called her repeatedly about his behavior, then demanded she come into class and see how he was behaving. Her son was, indeed, having a tantrum when the mother arrived, because the teacher had told him that his behavior was "an embarrassment to the class and to her." After numerous meetings, the school expelled the boy for fighting with another child. Eventually, he ended up being home schooled for six months, then placed in a private school, which the school district refused to pay for. Legal proceedings resulted, and now the district does pay for part of the child's tuition. And his mother says he's much happier in a school where his idiosyncrasies are better understood.

"It was obvious from the beginning that they couldn't cope," the mother says now, about three years later. "But they wouldn't send anybody for training, and they really seemed to just want to get (my son) out of the class."

Still, most parents of children on the spectrum are currently opting for inclusion when possible. Unless the child's behavior is so extreme that it would be disruptive to the class on a constant basis, and the child would not benefit from being in the class, inclusion has become very much the desired course of action for most parents of children with AS.

Does that mean you're a failure if you opt for something other than inclusion? Of course not. Does it mean that you should fight tooth and nail for inclusion if you think it's the right thing for your child? Yes, it does.

There's only one right way for your child, and that's the way your child is going to feel most comfortable, get the best education and most successfully socialize with his classmates. And only you know your child well enough to know what you want. Don't let me or anyone else tell you that something you know is wrong is the best course for your child, because it's not.

For my son, inclusion is the right choice. He has been included since kindergarten, is now in sixth grade, and has thrived on it. He's made a few friends at school – not a lot, but some – and does well in his classes. The other children in his classes know him so well, having been with him since first grade, that his stimming doesn't even register on their radar screens anymore. Occasionally, the student sitting next to him in class will nudge Josh, tell him he's humming or flapping his fingers, and that he should stop. And Josh does. But it's not a source of teasing for him anymore, and that's a huge help.

Inclusion has served my child well. It may or may not serve yours as well. With variables like the school district, the available help, the classroom teacher and (especially) the child in each case, there's no way to predict from the outside how the student will react. Even with testing, observation and a team of specialists monitoring your child's progress, you can't be sure that you're making the right decision. Life is a crapshoot; you take your best guess.

But if you look deep into your child's eyes and see what's there, I'm willing to bet you'll know what to do.

Remember That Person You're Married To?

*Y*OU SPEND A LOT OF TIME CARING FOR your child, and a child with Asperger Syndrome can require more care than most. Sometimes, it's difficult to remember the other people in your life. Yourself, for example.

But if the first person in your orbit who falls by the wayside because of the time and effort it takes to live with AS is you, the second is often your spouse. No statistics are available on the divorce rate among AS parents, but a marriage that deals with the typical stresses of life plus Asperger Syndrome is under more pressure than one without AS in the family.

In other words, you have to pay attention to that person you promised to love, honor and cherish. The one standing next to you in your wedding pictures. The one next to you when you go to sleep at night.

See? You remember. Your spouse.

There's no question that AS can be a strain on a marriage – even on a strong marriage. Some parents get through the difficult periods in fine shape; others don't get through them at all. It's hard for one partner to concentrate on the constant adjustments that need to be made with the care of a child with Asperger Syndrome, while the other's focus is more on keeping the family afloat financially. Even when both parents are working outside the home, it's usually one or the other who handles school issues, doctor appointments, homework problems and after-school transportation. These jobs are rarely distributed evenly.

For the parent whose focus is on work, in order to keep a roof over the family and food on the table, the problem is often one of *guilt*. This parent sees the other constantly in motion, immersed in AS issues, attending support group meetings and communicating with school personnel, and wonders if paying the bills is enough.

The other parent, who is hip-deep in AS issues, has to contend with *resentment* and *burnout*. Often, this is the parent who feels the weight of AS most strongly, and sees a spouse as having the easier of the two loads, whether that is true or not. This is also the parent most likely to overload on AS, or to become so ingrained in the condition and the community that has formed around it that it's impossible to pull out at the end of the day and be "just" a wife or a husband again.

Invariably, two people who started out together because they felt the same way find their lives going in separate directions. That can lead to the kind of problems no married person wants to face.

Ellen Lemma's marriage wasn't in strong shape before her son was diagnosed with AS, and it split up two weeks later. While Ellen says the divorce was unrelated to the diagnosis, and that it would have happened anyway, it has made raising her son Christopher, who is now eight years old, more difficult.

"It wasn't the Asperger Syndrome that broke up the marriage," she says. "But it's been different, because almost as soon as we had the diagnosis, the marriage was over. It was just about the same time."

"Any time you have any stress in a family, there might be marital problems," says Dr. Jed Baker. "Whether it's a financial stressor, or a chronic illness of somebody in the family, a loss, any major stressor can put stress on a family, including a marriage. And if you have a chronic issue, such as a child who has a lot of challenging behaviors, it's going to take away from the adult time parents can spend together. The behaviors cause direct stress."

There are a number of ways in which AS can create stress on a marriage. For example, many of the parents I've interviewed (although certainly not all) believed that they or their spouse might have "a touch" of Asperger Syndrome themselves, and therefore might have carried a genetic component that led to the child's AS.

That can be devastating in many different areas. If you believe that you "caused" your child's AS, it's not unusual to feel guilty about it. Of course, it isn't something you intentionally passed on, or in all likelihood even something you knew you had to pass on, but a lot of AS parents fall victim to feelings of direct responsibility for their children's disabilities.

Possibly worse is the type of stress that can be placed on a marriage when your spouse believes you are the "carrier." This can complicate matters because one parent feels accused of causing the child's problems, and also thinks that there might be something in his own behavior that indicates a disability.

"It can be a problem if one parent is saying, 'you're the reason my son has this, because you have it, too,'" says Dr. Baker. If the child's mother believes his father might have symptoms of AS, the father can feel tension, even if (sometimes especially if) she doesn't say so out loud.

Often, when a child is diagnosed with Asperger Syndrome, one parent (or both) goes into "denial," assuming that the diagnosis is incorrect. It's a lot to absorb all at once, and because AS is not an "obvious" condition, sometimes parents try their best to believe that nothing is wrong, or at least that it's not the lifelong condition a doctor is describing.

Elizabeth Roberts, PSYD, is a clinical neuropsychologist who specializes in children with Asperger Syndrome. When it's time for her to give a diagnosis of AS or another autism spectrum disorder, she knows it's possible that one or both parents will not want to hear what she has to say.

"There are different kinds of denial. One is fear of the 'autism word,' so they're going to call it nonverbal learning disability. Well, that doesn't cover the whole story," she says. "So, while I'm interviewing them, I'm assessing their receptiveness to what I think I'm going to be saying to them. Usually, the person in denial is the father, although not always. Many times they're physicians. They don't even come to the feedback sessions. We're telling these people a momentously important thing, and they're too busy to come to the feedback; it's mind-boggling."

Giving parents a diagnosis, then, can be tricky. Dr. Roberts says she can't go too far with a parent who isn't ready to discuss the possibility of autism or AS, a condition they may never have heard of before.

"It's like taking someone's temperature; you're always gauging how much they can handle," she says. "One of the secrets of psychotherapy in general is timing. No matter how truthful something is that you want to say, you're just causing damage if you say it at the wrong time. You're giving them a little bit of what you think, but if you feel like they can't handle it at that moment, you're going to back off a little. You're kind of treading water or moving back and forth to gauge how much they can handle."

When a parent is in denial, it's difficult to discuss options. And if one parent (usually the one who leaps into research immediately and becomes an instant expert on AS) is anxious to move on to the battles to come, but the other is insisting this is "just a phase," stress in the relationship can be very strong.

"Then there's the issue if a father is accused of having a touch of Asperger Syndrome, he may not want to acknowledge that his son has it," Dr. Baker says, "because then he might have to acknowledge that there's something going on with him, too."

Arguments between parents who disagree on the diagnosis, and therefore the treatment, of a child with AS can be a major source of tension in a marriage, and sometimes the tension overwhelms the rest of the relationship. There are divorces, there is family counseling, couples counseling and, worst of all, unspoken resentments between parents who don't deal with the emotional issues at all.

"At the beginning, it was very tough," Lori Shery recalls about the months after her son's diagnosis. "(My husband) didn't want to accept it. It had an effect on our marriage. It had an effect on parenting in general, and it was tough. Finally, he's accepted it. He'll even tell people he has an autistic son. That's a big step for him. It took me eight months to get through my mourning period. It took him two years. He was resentful of a lot of things. He was resentful that his son had a serious disability. He was resentful of the fact that I spent so much time and energy dealing with it. He was resentful of the fact that it took a lot of our resources. And it really ran the household. Everything was built around Adam's therapies and Adam's bad days."

Lori works with a good number of parents, and she is distressed with the effect she sees on their marriages. Denial – usually, but not always, from the father – takes a toll, as does the issue of one parent spending more time with the child with AS than the other. This can cause tension both ways, as the stay-at-home parent may resent the other's contact with the "non-AS" world, and the parent who works outside the home can resent the amount of attention and time the child with AS receives, and feel a little guilty about that.

"You have to mind the marriage also. Otherwise it can disintegrate," Lori warns. "If I could give you a percentage of the parents that I know and work with, I would say maybe thirty percent have gotten divorced, at least. It's a large percentage. It's a really large percentage. It makes me so sad. For any of those

I have asked, 'Did the Asperger Syndrome come into play there?,' the answer is always yes."

Luckily, Lori's husband Steven worked through his denial, and together, they have done remarkable work with Adam. Lori and Steven also try to get out by themselves once a week, and the family spends most warm-weather weekends boating together.

Because I am the work-at-home parent in our family, I spend more time with my son and daughter than my wife does. In most cases, however, the mother is the parent who stays home, while the father works outside the house. Dr. Baker says that no matter which parent stays home and which leaves for work, the discrepancy in the time spent with a child with AS can cause friction between parents, even if it's unspoken.

"If you have to sit and listen to a tantrum for four hours after you come home from work, there's going to be a direct stress," he says. "Part of what happens, too, is that in many cases it's the mom who spends the most time, and whoever spends the most time with the youngster is going to have the most challenges. Kids might be on their best behavior when Daddy comes home and they haven't seen Daddy all day. The novelty is exciting and interesting, and they want to please Daddy because Daddy's not around so much."

For some parents, like Ellen Silva, whose son Sean has AS, it's a question of understanding the daily routine better than her husband, who works outside the house. "(My husband) doesn't get (Asperger Syndrome) as much as I do," she says. "It's the little things that he doesn't see every day. Sean will not get dressed unless you physically take out his clothes. My husband said, 'I sent him up to get dressed, and I go up two hours later and he hasn't gotten anything done.' I said, 'Did you take his clothes out?' No. But Sean won't come back down and say 'will you take my clothes out?' Both of them are wrong. You want to say to Sean, 'You're nine years old, you should be able to dress yourself,' but I guess I choose my battles.

I figure it this way: I know he goes to school neat every day because I take his clothes out. Everything matches. Everything he puts on fits."

Ellen says she and her husband make sure to have a night out regularly. Luckily, Sean has a teenage sister who can babysit when necessary and gets along well with her brother. But for any couple whose child has AS, it's important to work harder than most at being a couple.

There is no magic formula for relieving the stress that AS can cause on a relationship. The same hard work that goes into raising children needs to be applied. Couples who were married for years before having children might have an easier time remembering the things they did to keep the relationship strong before the focus shifted to smaller, more needy people.

The key is remembering that you *are* a couple. You're two people who committed to each other before you ever heard of Asperger Syndrome. You've been a couple all this time, even if it feels like your only roles are Mom and Dad. Even when dealing with school districts, child study teams, psychologists, psychiatrists, neurologists, social workers and speech therapists is more than you can handle. Even when your spouse comes home from work grumpy because of something that happened at the office, and doesn't want to hear about the meltdown you had to endure over science homework. You're still a couple.

Given that fact, the next thing to do is make sure you have time to *be* a couple. Married people tend to forget that alone time is important for them, too, and when they're not at work, they often fill their time with separate interests and family activities that involve the children. That's fine, but there has to be separation once in a while, to just be two people who love each other.

AS parents who persevere tend to recognize that fact. Even when finding a babysitter is difficult because of the child's behavior patterns, or the cost, they find the time to get away together for a movie, dinner, or just a quiet walk or an afternoon in the park. Dr. Baker says that kind of commitment is very important to a marriage, particularly one under stress from a disability in the family.

"Not everybody can afford that, but people need a respite, people need babysitters, people need time. The quality time can only happen if people have somebody who can take care of their kid for a while," he says. "Sometimes graduate students in special education have offered to babysit because it was a way for them to gain direct experience working with youngsters with different kinds of educational challenges. I know parents who have advertised at graduate programs in education at different colleges in order to get babysitters."

Sometimes, just the notion of time away from your child can seem daunting. Some parents become so engrossed in the care of their children with AS that they almost reach the point of obsession; *every* decision seems to be a crucial one, and every moment must be overseen, usually by that parent. Sneaking away for time to yourself and your spouse can seem like "cheating," as if devoting any time to anything other than your child is wrong. It's not unusual to feel guilty.

That doesn't mean you shouldn't get away; on the contrary: if you're that involved, a break is even more important. And it's not just important to your spouse; it's important to you. Maintaining your identity separate from being "Mom" or "Dad" is vital. Part of that is being "husband," "wife" or "lover," and that's what this kind of "away time" is all about.

A good, reliable babysitter is absolutely essential for parents of children with AS, even up to the early teenage years in some cases. If that places too much of a financial burden on you, ask if a relative or close friend, someone the child knows well (and who knows your child well) can pinch hit for an evening. Babysitting "co-ops" are also a good solution: parents of children with similar issues offer to alternate nights when one child or another can stay at one couple's home while another couple spends time together without their child.

And where do you go from there? Any place you want. Any place you can. If it's a movie you're dying to see, a restaurant you've always wanted to try or an old, familiar place that you used to call "home" before you were a parent, that's your business. Some couples go on a "date" just to remember what it feels like to do that. Others search the newspaper for exciting events that will take place nearby, to get a feeling of doing something new again. It doesn't matter what you choose to do; what's important is that you're alone, and you're together.

Don't set rules that you won't be able to follow. Some couples make it a strict policy not to talk about their children when they're out on a "date." Others don't feel this will enhance the evening. Sometimes, you do need to discuss what's going on out of the child's earshot. As long as you're not arguing about some point of your child's care, you can discuss it and have a pleasant break at the same time.

My wife and I are movie people. We spent much of our pre-parenting years at the movies, and actually retreated to a movie theatre when my wife was just beginning to go into labor with Josh. It was 95 degrees out, and the theatre was air-conditioned! Besides, they were showing (I swear!) *Parenthood*. It seemed appropriate.

Since Josh and his sister were born, though, we see most films on cassette or DVD, and get to the theatre maybe one tenth of the times we used to. It usually doesn't matter to us, but we do miss the experience, and occasionally ask a relative or a sitter to take over for us when there's a film we're especially interested in seeing on the big screen.

Those evenings are special, and not just because we're both glad to return to something we used to love so dearly. Being by ourselves, being able to talk to each other without interruption (generally on the subject of "Dungeons and Dragons," which is Josh's latest obsession), remembering why we were interested in spending the rest of our lives together in the first place – and seeing a movie that's actually made for adults – make the time pass quickly. When there's a sitter at home, the time passes more quickly, since the meter is running the whole time we're out. But it's worth the money.

When the kids were very young, my wife sometimes felt a little guilty leaving them, even for a few hours. She'd turn to me ten minutes after we left the house and say, "I miss them." That doesn't happen so much anymore, since the kids are older and don't really mind (or, in Josh's case, notice) if we're out of the house. And she realizes that a break is important, perhaps more so to me than to her, because I get the after-school hours as well as the evenings with both our children.

What's really interesting is that Josh has become a movie person, too. In a couple of years, we'll want to see the same movies on occasion. But he may make us sit in a different area of the theatre. Parents can be so embarrassing.

Sibling Revelry

"Mom always liked you best."

– Tommy Smothers

*W*HEN MY SON WAS SPECIFICALLY NOT invited back to his "typical-setting" summer camp in 1999, he began attending the Harbor Haven camp in West Orange, New Jersey, a day camp facility for children with autism spectrum disorders, among others, about forty-five minutes from our house. When we went to the orientation day before camp began, our daughter Eve, who was six years old at the time, saw the swimming pool, the arts and crafts, the baseball diamonds, the volleyball courts and the basketball hoops. She heard the camp's director, Robyn Tanne, explain the schedule of the day, which included games, bicycle riding, swimming and half-day trips.

During the ride home, Eve was quiet for a long time, and then looked at me in the driver's seat.

"Daddy," she said, "I want to go to Asperger Syndrome camp, too."

Raising a child with Asperger Syndrome who has no brothers or sisters is difficult. Raising one who has a sibling, or more, is ... different. It may not be easier or harder, but it certainly isn't the same.

The difficult issues for siblings aren't all that different from those for spouses. A large amount of attention, time and affection is spent on the child with AS, and unless parents are very careful to be evenhanded (and even sometimes when they are), the sibling, older or younger, can feel neglected. Sibling rivalry is intense enough when there *aren't* special needs and special solutions in the family. The problem is compounded by the fact that the person who feels neglected is not an adult, and can't fully understand the situation.

"It would be great to have a support group for siblings," says Elizabeth Roberts, PSYD. "They get embarrassed. That's really hard. They will get a special set of rules because everybody's created differently: 'how come he's allowed to eat hot dogs every night,' and that stuff."

Also, because AS is a series of behaviors that are tied very closely to emotions, and because meltdowns can affect an entire family's day, siblings often feel that the child with AS can "get away" with behavior that would surely earn the sibling severe punishment.

It's beyond obvious to say that it's important to spend quality time with the neurotypical child as well as the child with AS. But sometimes, that's not as easy as it might seem. Between meetings of the social skills group, visits to the doctor, the inevitable difficulties with one teacher or another and just trying to get through a typical day, the raising of a child with AS can seem to take over a household.

That can be very difficult on the child who doesn't have special issues. Younger ones especially don't understand the family dynamic, and can't possibly grasp the concepts of neurodevelopmental delays, involuntary stimming, behavior caused by differences in the brain or even the amount of time it takes to drive to the doctor's office and back when they need to be home for a particular cartoon show. Explaining why things are the way they are can take a good deal of effort, and some talent.

Birth order can play a part in sibling rivalry, whether there are AS issues or not. I am the younger of two sons, and remember vividly how I felt growing up: it was clear that my parents were favoring my brother, paying more attention to his accomplishments. I always had to work twice as hard to be noticed.

From a perspective a few decades down the line, I realize that is all untrue. My parents were, in fact, fanatically scrupulous about being evenhanded with my brother and me. But from a nine-year-old's point of view, logic isn't necessarily the most highly developed resource.

Now imagine how that nine-year-old would feel if the parents – out of necessity – really *were* paying more attention to the other child. If, because the other child needed more help, more of Mom and Dad's time and effort had to be devoted to him, and not to the sibling. A child doesn't understand cause and effect – he just knows he's not getting the attention (and, it would seem, the love) his sibling is receiving from his parents.

In some ways, birth order will play a role in the rivalry and difficulties siblings experience. And while it's hard for the sibling who feels neglected, the child with AS often senses that he's the reason for tension in the house, and that will affect him emotionally, as well.

Maggie Casciato's son Tom, who has AS, is now twenty-two years old, and his brother James is nineteen. Their animosity has continued for a good number of years, and it's something Maggie says must be confronted.

"From the time Tom realized he was different, his little brother realized it, too," she says. "At the beginning, it was outright embarrassment. At one point, for a couple of years they went to the same school, and that was really embarrassing for the younger one. He wouldn't go to the bus stop with (Tom), and that was at the age when all his friends were making fun of (Tom), and he would join in. It never got totally worked out. The two of them tolerate each other, but they barely talk to each other. They're certainly not friends. It's going to take an awful lot of maturity on both sides for them to be good friends."

Not every situation is that serious. Sometimes, the usual sibling issues of attention and care given are all that arise, AS or no AS. When the child with AS is older, the issues may be different than for those families in which the child with AS is a younger sibling. In the latter case, a child who has received all the care and attention an only child enjoys might be more resentful of the littler, more demanding sibling.

"We do parent training and sometimes design programs for siblings who are experiencing jealousy over all the attention a sibling with a disability receives," says Dr. Jed Baker. "It's probably a little easier for a younger sibling who never had the privilege of being the only one."

Parents whose first child has AS might be a little more protective, or even nervous, about a second or third child. Because AS is usually unforeseen, parents who have been "once bitten" might look a little too closely for signs of autistic behavior in younger children.

Lori Shery remembers a specific set of circumstances that distracted her from looking for signs of AS when her second son was born.

"When I was in my first trimester with Zachary, I started having contractions and bleeding. I was confined to bed rest flat on my back for three weeks," she recalls. "Then, a few weeks later, I got chicken pox. I got a terrible case of it. The doctors were very concerned, and I ended up having five ultrasounds because they were worried about Zachary. They told me when he was born that if he was pockmarked, it was going to be bad news and if he wasn't, chances are it would be okay. Well, he was beautiful when he was born. But when he was four months old, he got shingles, and you can only get shingles if you've been infected with chicken pox. So what we were watching for with

Zachary was mostly effects from the chicken pox. But after we got a diagnosis for Adam, and Zachary was already born, yes, I watched for things with Zachary. I knew he wasn't like Adam. He was very different from Adam. I really didn't think he was going to be on the autism spectrum. But I was watching for other things."

Parents despair over sibling rivalry even when they're being as evenhanded as possible. And while they can explain to both children (or in some cases, all the children) that they don't love one more than the other, it's hard to fight that perception when a child with AS demands considerably more attention and obvious planning than a neurotypical child.

Our daughter Eve has always been understanding about her brother, but it does bother her now that they attend the same school, when other children make fun of him. She told me just the other day that it was "embarrassing," and that she didn't know how to react when she saw kids copying Josh's stimming or his facial expressions.

"What do you do when you see it?" I asked her.

"Usually, I don't do anything," she admitted. "I don't know the kids who are doing it, and I don't want to talk to them."

Embarrassment is natural with children, and it's especially prevalent in kids from age nine through the teenage years. The problem will only get worse for Eve, as she'll eventually be embarrassed not just by Joshua, but by *everything*, especially her parents. Luckily, after this year, she and Josh will be in the same school only for two more years, and that will be in high school, when they're both (gasp!) teenagers.

Sometimes, siblings of children with AS get along just fine with their less typical brother or sister. For example, Ellen Silva's daughter, who is eight years older than her brother with AS, sometimes babysits for Sean when Ellen and her husband need to take some time off.

"She's very good with him," Ellen reports. "She's eight years older: she's a senior in high school. I think the hardest part of her going off to college next year will be leaving her brother. She's his protector. She'll talk to him sometimes about social skills when she sees him doing something really inappropriate. She'll try to explain it to him in a kid way. To him, she is a kid, even though she's an adult, too."

In fact, Ellen says her daughter's experience with Sean has led her to want to help people like him. "My daughter's guidance counselor in high school told me that one of the reasons she's interested in going into the medical field is because of her brother," Ellen says. "(My daughter) wouldn't tell me, but she'd tell her guidance counselor."

When children are young, they are less likely to experience serious feelings of rivalry or resentment, because they might not understand, or even notice, that their sibling with AS is receiving extra care. As they grow, these feelings become more likely, because the children start to understand their roles in the family, and become aware that more time and attention is being spent on one child, out of necessity. But they rarely recognize the necessity, and even when they do, it doesn't make them feel any better.

"These two kids don't even talk to each other," Maggie Casciato says of her sons. "It's a serious problem that we have to settle, a real antagonism between the two of them. We're not quite sure what it is. (James) is more like a typical teenager, the younger one, but he has some of his own issues. We've been in family therapy with him. It's a serious situation. They both antagonize each other. They've learned to tolerate each other."

It's helpful to explain the condition to the sibling who doesn't have AS as soon as he or she is old enough to understand. The more the neurotypical sibling can be assured that his/her brother or sister isn't acting that way just to be annoying, the better the chances are the "typical" sibling will understand.

Such an explanation would be much the same as the kind of presentation done in a classroom for neurotypical classmates, but obviously on a much more intimate scale. You know your child, and you know what he or she can understand. Explain about AS in terms that make sense to the child. Tell him or her that the sibling who has AS is not "sick," and reassure your neurotypical child that the brother or sister is in no danger.

Children have a difficult time differentiating between illnesses that kill and conditions that are medically related, but not threatening to health. It's important your neurotypical child, especially if he or she is younger, understand that this is not a "catching" condition, and that it is not a scary thing.

But AS will cause your child to act differently than most, and the neurotypical sibling has to be able to understand that. Use words like "different" and "unusual," but don't refer to the neurotypical child as "normal," or use terms like "sick" and "well" to make the distinction.

It's equally important to take the neurotypical child's feelings into account. Make sure you emphasize that Mom and Dad don't love one child more than the other, but that sometimes the child with AS might require more time and attention to get through times and tasks the neurotypical child might be able to accomplish more easily. In other words, some things are going to take longer. They're going to require more attention from Mom or Dad. That doesn't mean (the sibling with AS) is stupid or doesn't understand; she or he just learns differently.

My daughter Eve is still struggling with her feelings about AS, but she and Josh are in many ways a typical brother and sister in the pre-teen years. They annoy each other for the sheer sport of it, and act surprised when their "game" gets out of hand. My wife and I would love to simply chalk it up to a "typical" aspect of their relationship, but the fact is, the constant bickering drives us just as crazy as it would the parents of two neurotypical children.

The irritation is just as real, only different.

What is obvious is that Eve knows that Josh isn't getting special treatment because their mother and I love him more, or because AS allows him to "get away" with things that she can't.

Even at age nine, she understands that Josh has some differences in the way he acts, and that other people aren't always going to understand them. This bothers her, but she hasn't yet determined how to be loyal to her brother and deal with the embarrassment he causes her at school.

That was a problem for Maggie Casciato's sons, and it hasn't been resolved to this day.

"We talked a lot about (James') relationship with Tom when we were in therapy with him," Maggie recalls. "(James) didn't want to talk about it, but my husband and I did. We felt that we didn't neglect him, because when he was little, we went to all his Little League games, took him to Scouts, and he was an altar boy. But in spite of all of that, he still acted out and rebelled. It could be that he just has a rebellious nature and it was aggravated by the fact that his brother was an embarrassment to him for so many years, and still is sometimes."

While the situation isn't openly hostile, Maggie does regret that her sons aren't close, and in fact seem to have trouble being in the same room.

"Even now, when the four of us are sitting at the dinner table, Tom will start to talk about something. Don and I are used to it now. We enjoy it when Tom starts to talk because he'll pontificate. He'll talk about movies, for example. That's his current passion. James will just sit there and roll his eyes. As much as Tom knows this information, it doesn't turn into a conversation very often. It is rare that the four of us get into a conversation, when somehow we get onto a topic that all four of us will talk about. It still is extremely unusual. This is one of the times my heart aches. Most of the time I'd rather not have the two of them together, because James will just be silent and sullen and make faces, and Tom will like to talk, but the two of them won't talk to each other."

As with everything else, the way siblings get along – with or without AS – is a matter of personality. Maggie's sons might not have been close even if Tom had been neurotypical, and other families find that one child's AS makes the others more protective, and in a way closer. There's no way of predicting.

What's important is to maximize the chances you have, and your best weapon is information. Help all your children understand about Asperger Syndrome and the way it affects the family member who has it. If your child with AS understands his condition, he can help explain. If not, he should probably understand as soon as it's appropriate for him to know. It's one thing to "come out" to the outside world, but explaining to your child with AS why people might treat him differently is simply a matter of following the Boy Scout motto: Be Prepared.

Share with the rest of your children as much information as your child with AS considers comfortable; it's not necessary to share personal details that will embarrass anyone. And, of course, make sure all the children get as close to equal treatment as time, personality, and AS will allow.

Allow yourself mistakes, because we all make them. Don't go out of your way to favor one child over the other, but realize that there will be a day or two along the line where it might, out of circumstance or necessity, happen. Apologize to the other children when it does, and move on. Nobody except your children expects you to be perfect.

It's common knowledge, finally, that no matter how evenhanded you manage to be, no matter how many different ways you bend over backwards to accommodate everyone, no matter how often you put your own life on hold to tend to others' needs, after all is said and done, you will still be wrong. Your children will all feel neglected, they are guaranteed to resent whatever effort you make, and they will undoubtedly end up complaining about you on some future-time analyst's couch.

After all, the parents are always wrong. Or maybe it just seems that way.

Sometimes, It's All Too Much

*N*EW PARENTS ARE OFTEN TOLD about the concept of "overload." New babies, they're told, will cry for baffling reasons, will keep their parents awake, will drive parents to distraction. When you reach "overload," you're supposed to put the baby in the crib, crying or not, and leave the room immediately, before your emotions and your sleep deprivation get the best of you.

New parents have nothing on the parents of children with Asperger Syndrome.

Because our children have less social capability than others, because they are given to behaviors that can seem rude, even obnoxious, they are capable of stress-inducing behavior far beyond the capabilities of neurotypical children.

Another way of saying all that is: no matter how good a parent you are, your child with AS can drive you crazy. You might as well face up to that now. There will be times when you'll lose your temper, when you'll say things you don't mean and when you do things you'll desperately want to take back.

In the words of psychologist Jed Baker, "welcome to the human race."

Sometimes, it seems as though Asperger Syndrome was designed specifically to drive parents up a wall. The insistence on ritual, the inability to understand inflection or idioms, the constant talk about arcane subjects – all these things conspire to chip away at even the most patient parent's composure until, by the end of the day, each of us is a quivering, mumbling ball of neuroses, worn to a frazzle by one of the people we love the most in this world. Or so it seems.

When Joshua has decided, particularly at bedtime, that he is "funny," and that he will begin telling jokes and riddles, taking everything literally for the sake of a laugh – or in any other way delaying the end of the evening – he has found exactly the button to push in my psyche to engender a response. The response generally isn't a positive one, but Josh doesn't seem to care much about that.

It is at that moment that I am especially glad my wife is there, since I can turn to her, say, "I'm going to walk the dog," and remove myself from the situation. Unless, of course, my spouse has the same look on her face that I have on mine, in which case someone has to suck it up and get the boy to brush his teeth. Luckily, my wife is a much more patient soul than I am.

It's not unusual for parents of children with AS or any other disorder to feel more stressed than others. In the course of our average day, we have more decisions to make, more problems to overcome, more obstacles to avoid. So we need a release that much more.

"You're not perfect," Dr. Baker says. "Parents of kids with disabilities often feel incompetent and powerless and often get depressed about themselves as parents. And that can carry over into the workplace, because 'if I don't feel like I'm a competent parent, maybe I'm not good at what I do, either.' You often see depression secondary to a child's problem. It's not just that parental depression causes behavior problems; it's often the reverse. Behavior problems in children can cause parental depression."

I can't tell you how to treat clinical depression (although a certified psychologist can), but I know how many parents of children with AS deal with their emotions. It's the trick of the "steam valve," the release that lets you escape the pressures of your day-to-day life and just be you for a while, a method of "recharging the batteries."

Some people go to the movies; others go bowling. Some close themselves in a room and read a book. It doesn't matter what form your "steam valve" takes, as long as it doesn't hurt anyone else. If you can enjoy yourself often enough, and for long enough, to make the rest of your day, week or month easier, you have found the proper outlet.

"I sing in two choruses, and I love it," says Maggie Casciato. "One's a church choir, and the other is called the Mendelssohn Choir. It's semi-pro type of chorus, and we do a lot of classical choral works. I love to sing, so two nights a week, I'm out singing. That's total therapy. Even when the kids were younger, my husband didn't mind. He would babysit the kids while I went out to sing."

Hobbies aren't necessary to fight the feeling of saturation, however. Some parents find that an evening at a support group for parents of children with AS, such as ASPEN, is immediately helpful – it provides an outlet to "vent" feelings that other adults don't understand, and to commiserate with the only peer group that can empathize completely about AS issues.

Some people don't just *join* support groups. Some people *start* support groups. When Maggie Casciato's son was diagnosed, AS wasn't nearly as well known as it is today, and having a child attached to the word "autism" was a frightening thought, one that most parents wouldn't even mention to friends. Maggie found her outlet when she met another mother whose child had special needs.

"It was just by chance at a birthday party for a friend of James' (her younger, neurotypical son)," Maggie says. "One of the mothers and I decided to go for a cup of coffee. We discovered that our older sons both had the diagnosis Atypical PDD. We both went, 'ah!' That's how we started our group, which was probably one of the first in the country for high-functioning autism."

Maggie organized a number of other parents whose children had high-functioning autism disorders, and when they had their first meeting, she had no idea how large the group would grow.

"It started out being called the Atypical PDD Support Group. Now it's called the Asperger Syndrome/PDD Support Group. We started ten years ago, and now, we just pared the list for this year, we have about 250 families and professionals on our list just in this part of Connecticut. We get between thirty and sixty people at our meetings," Maggie says. "At first we wondered if there was anybody else in this area with that diagnosis, and at our first meeting, we had fourteen people, and we were thrilled. Now, we've got hundreds."

By the same token, Lori Shery says co-founding ASPEN from her living room in New Jersey was a means of dealing with her son Adam's AS and an outlet for herself, a way for her to help others and take on responsibility outside her own family.

"I'm a good listener. The one thing that I want to give parents – and none of us has a crystal ball, I don't have one about my child, you don't have one about yours – is to give them hope," Lori says. "Most of the time, when parents contact me, they're crying and they're devastated. They need someone to say to them, 'It's going to be OK.' When I explain to them it's going to be OK, I also tell them, 'It's not going to go away, they're always going to have it, they're not going to be the same as other people. But they can do this, and they can do that, this is how we can help them.' And when I get off the phone with them, they usually say, 'You've made me feel much better. You've made me feel there's a light at the end of the tunnel.'"

Other parents find ways of releasing their tension outside support groups. Ellen Silva and her husband go bowling once a week. One mother I spoke to asks a friend to watch her son, then goes to a Saturday afternoon movie and escapes with a bucket of popcorn every once in a while. There are hang gliders, sailboat enthusiasts, baseball fans, avid readers, hobbyists, collectors, workaholics and nap-takers whose children have AS. The important thing is to find the outlet that works for you, and then religiously devote the time to indulging it.

I write screenplays and novels to exercise my mind's fantasies, but sometimes AS enters into that world, too. The hero of my mystery novels has a son with Asperger Syndrome, but in his dealings, he too makes mistakes, realizes them, and tries to correct them. Sometimes in make-believe, we find ways to work through our real-life problems.

"One way to fight that feeling of powerlessness and incompetence is to talk about it, and find out that it *isn't* just you," says Dr. Jed Baker. "Your child does have some challenges, and it's not that what you're doing isn't effective, it's that it's not always going to be effective in the face of your child's challenges."

But you have to realize there will be times when you're going to lose your temper. Asperger Syndrome is a condition that would cause Mother Teresa to lose her temper if she were subjected to it every hour of every day. You aren't a failure because you can't cope with *every* situation, or even because you can't cope with any situation at the end of a long day. It's the way you deal with your lapses in judgment or your impulsive moments that matters.

"I don't have a lot of breaks," says Sharon Graebener. "I was just thinking to myself, maybe I'll ask my mother if she can take him for a few hours so we can go to the movies or something. I need a break from Max. And it isn't really Max; it's the situation. It's just give, give, give. And if you don't, the kid falls apart. You have to take care of the children, you have to constantly speak to them, constantly explain life to them."

Part of the trick is in words: think of AS not as an obstacle, or a condition, or a problem, but as a *challenge*. It might not mean anything more than a semantic change in your thinking, but the differentiation is important. A *problem* is something you have to solve, or you're a failure. An *obstacle* is something that someone has thrown in your way to impede your progress. A *condition* is a chronic, debilitating situation that will ultimately defeat you no matter what you do.

A *challenge*, on the other hand, is something that exists for the expressed purpose of being dealt with. It is something that can be – if not overcome – examined, searched for weaknesses, plotted against and engaged. It can be battled and, in some cases, it can be defeated outright. But the best thing about a challenge is that it doesn't require you to change who you are or how you live; it requires that you do some things differently to accommodate your situation. In order to deal with a challenge, you learn new ways to cope with familiar situations, you devise new strategies to shore up your weaknesses and turn them into strengths. Does this sound familiar?

"It's so challenging," says Dr. Baker. "You can't fall into the trap of overgeneralizing that you're a bad parent because of one or two incidences, or worse yet, that you're a bad person and an incompetent person. A lot of losing your temper comes from feeling powerless and incompetent. That's why people scream; they feel like nothing else is going to work, or nothing's going to work. They lose their temper, just like a kid who gets frustrated because he can't get to the next level on the Gameboy. It isn't about you being a bad parent; it is the normal course."

So how do you deal with the challenge of everyday life with AS? Some people are more gifted with patience than others, and they're usually the ones whose children don't have Asperger Syndrome. That's just an observation, not a scientific fact.

There's no magic formula. Some parents are encouraged just by the fact that they aren't the only ones who lose their temper once in a while. At support group meetings, new AS parents often remark that they "didn't know everybody reacted like that." Well, everybody does, sooner or later.

In other cases, parents find help in the simplest forms of self-discipline: if your temper is running short, and your child won't stop the behavior that's driving you to distraction, leave the room, pure and simple. Before the incident becomes an *incident*, leave the room. You need time to regroup, and you can certainly come up with a better strategy with a few minutes of quiet time to think.

"I give myself time-out," says Ellen Silva. "When I'm really ready to lose it, most of the times it's not his fault. I will tell him Mommy's in time-out. And I'll go in my room, I'll read a book, I'll go on the computer. Sean will come downstairs giggling because Mommy's in time-out. He knows to leave me alone until I come out. He thinks it's funny, but that's the way I phrased it to him, because it's not his fault. I am at the end of my rope."

Sharon Graebener says: "I read a lot. We go shopping. I go to Target and buy myself one thing. When I was younger, and on my own, I traveled; I lived in California for a while. All the stuff that thrills other people just doesn't do it for me anymore. We went to New York at Christmas time to see the tree; we went to a museum. We spend a lot of time together as a family. That fills me up. That's all I care about."

Those of us who have a spouse, a partner or just another adult in the room can rely on that person when the chips are down (or our dander is up). We can do "tag-team parenting," which allows for one parent to pass the baton to the other when the end of the rope is being reached. And it's not the least bit unusual for the behavior that drives one parent absolutely up a wall to have no effect whatsoever on the other. Nature can be kind, even when playing a joke of its own.

"Fortunately with Steven and me, given the same situation, on any particular day, one of us will stay calm while the other is losing it," Lori Shery reports. "So if I'm the one who's gotten really aggravated, I'll just walk into another room and say, 'I've had it. I'm not dealing with this,' and he'll go in and deal with it. We do the good cop/bad cop routine. Do I feel guilty afterwards? Only if I've said something that I regret saying. There are times that I get really angry with Adam because he has aggravated me and he says, 'But I didn't know.' I'll realize he really didn't know and that is part of the disorder. When any parent says to me, 'You know, I said this to my kid, or I've done this,' I always tell them, 'You know what? All the other parents do it, too.' We all do the same stuff; we say the same stuff."

When that "stuff" becomes too frequent, or your temper turns violent, it's time to find professional help. Don't wait until someone is physically hurt, or your relationship with your child has been damaged beyond repair. Even discipline has to be handled with love in parenting, or the consequences for both parent and child can be severe.

For most of us, though, that time never comes. We find our way through the rough spots, we deal with the overload, we face our *challenge* in a new way every day. It's like I always tell Josh: there's nothing wrong with making a mistake; the problem is making the *same* mistake over and over. That means you haven't learned anything from the experience.

Find your outlet. Discover that steam valve and use it when you need it. Or use it when you can steal a few minutes, to ensure that you won't need it later on. Deal with your child honestly and explain why the thing that he's doing is driving you crazy. But remember: these are kids with Asperger Syndrome, and most of them are very intelligent. Telling them what drives you up a wall might just be inviting them to try it again, just to see what will happen.

There's no secret formula to get you through the tough times; there's just your own resourcefulness, an attribute that will be frequently tested by your dealings with AS. But if you can gauge yourself, feel when your temper is being tested, know when to disengage and live to fight another day, you'll be two steps ahead of the rest of us who are still trying to figure it all out. A sense of self-knowledge is important; it gives us the advantage over our *challenge*. If we understand our own drives and difficulties well enough, we should be able to deal with the irritation and frustration the *challenge* can cause. It's strictly a case of turning down the emotional thermostat when necessary, which sounds easier than it is to do. But it can be done.

All you need is what you already have: an understanding of yourself and your child, and the capacity to escape every once in a while, even if it is just into the pages of a book. Even if it's a book like this one.

In other words, from a quote attributed to Franklin D. Roosevelt: when you find yourself at the end of your rope, tie a knot and hang on.

The Moments You Dread

I MUST PREFACE THIS NEXT EXAMPLE BY saying: things have gotten better.

This is what it used to be like to go out to eat with my son: hours before we left the house, we would have to make sure Josh was alerted that the family would be eating in a restaurant that night. After a half hour of arguments about how it would be better if we ordered Chinese food to take out, it would sink in to Josh that there was no escaping his fate. He'd have to leave his home to seek sustenance.

Then, still before leaving, the negotiating over the appropriate restaurant would begin. Since Josh's eating choices are, let's say, not incredibly broad, we would be limited to those establishments whose menus included beef hot dogs, fried chicken, or pasta, preferably overcooked and available with butter and parmesan cheese, but not Alfredo sauce, because that would be too easy.

We'd start by suggesting a place Josh hadn't been to before, but that suggestion wouldn't last very long, and was being offered with the kind of eternal optimism only parents can muster. We knew it would be the diner, or the one Italian restaurant Josh consents to enter. Usually, our daughter Eve would complain that we always went to the same two places, and Josh would get upset. We'd promise Eve she could choose the restaurant next time, and make a mental note to find somewhere else for Josh to be that night.

Then there was the drive to the restaurant. With Josh and Eve in the back seat, the argument over where we were eating – which we foolish parents believed had been settled – would continue and, more often than not, degenerate into some sort of physical confrontation. To be fair, Eve raised her hands just as often as Joshua, but it was inevitable that both sets of parental jaws would be tightly clenched by the time the car pulled into a parking spot.

Once inside the restaurant, we'd make sure that our children did not sit next to each other, so as to decrease the probability of continued violence. There would be the customary fighting over the menus, as if Josh would ever order anything but what he'd had at this particular restaurant every time before. Then, the comments after ordering: "How long does it take to make spaghetti?" "Will it be much longer?" "Do we get bread before the food comes?" All within the first five minutes.

When the unfortunate soul assigned to our table would ("finally!" Josh would add) arrive with our orders, more nit-picking would result. If there were parsley anywhere on the plate, the meal was ruined. If one food was (gasp!) touching another food, same result. If the water glasses were foolish enough to have lemon slices in them, it was akin to an international incident. One way or another, there would be some flaw – the sauce is the wrong color, the chicken isn't fried properly, the French fries are too crunchy, or not crunchy enough – that wouldn't necessarily doom the meal, but would always keep the tension level at our table high.

Josh would bolt his food, once it was properly altered, in roughly eight seconds, and then, while the rest of us ate our meals, he would roll his eyes, put his head down on the table and pretend to sleep, lean on one of us (or any family member masochistic enough to join us for dinner out), ask when he could leave the table and generally make a pain of himself until we'd let him go into the parking lot to watch the cars, or if the restaurant had a video game, endow him with enough quarters to last the twenty minutes or so until the rest of the family would be ready to leave. Dessert was out of the question; restaurants don't generally offer Oreos, the only after-meal treat Josh found suitable. So we'd all forgo dessert and leave with a sense of relief for us and everyone else in the room

Then there was the drive home. See paragraph above, re: the drive to the restaurant. Add a level of frustration having accumulated since the initial ride, and the idea that Josh was probably missing, or about to miss, the beginning of the next desperately important television show he insisted on seeing every night. Many teeth were gnashed. You get the idea.

In all, Josh's initial suggestion of ordering in usually sounded logical after we returned home from a restaurant.

Not all parents of children on the autism spectrum will admit it, but there's at least one activity, one situation, that gives them the chills. It's not the kind of moment that actually scares us (we'll get to that later), but it's the kind of thing we *know* is going to be uncomfortable, that we'll have to gear ourselves up just to endure, and we wonder if it will be worth the effort.

Pressure is no stranger to AS parents. But when we know that a difficult situation is on the horizon, we can deal with it in one of two ways: we can despair, grit our teeth and hope to endure, or we can capitalize on the opportunity, help to teach our children a new skill, and plan to avoid a few roadblocks along the way.

It's easy to say we should have a positive attitude in such situations, but besides being parents of children with AS, we're also human. So, like our children, sometimes we have to plan ahead to have a positive attitude.

Dr. Jed Baker says: "I've had parents who, before their youngsters go to a birthday party, will call the host parent and say, 'look, this is what may happen.' I have a client, for example, who has a lot of sensory issues, and every time she hears the Happy Birthday song, and there are a lot of kids around, it's very over-stimulating and she screams and can't tolerate it, and wants to leave. It's disruptive to the other kid's birthday, of course. Yet, part of the treatment in a way is for her to eventually be desensitized to that, so you want her to ride it out. The parent needs to make a deal with the parent of the child whose birthday it is, and let them know that this could happen, are you okay? We sit back a little bit, and if the child screams, we don't (immediately take her) away, we kind of hold through it for a little while."

Josh has a sensitivity to certain sounds; corduroy and other materials in clothing will send him up a wall. This is difficult in school, and whenever we take him out shopping, to the movies, or to eat. This is a situation that can't be helped with pre-planning; we don't know when someone is going to pass him in the street wearing a pair of pants that will make the offending sound.

The only training that can be done ahead of time is to give Josh an alternative reaction to flapping his arms, putting his hands over his ears, rolling his eyes back in his head and hopping up and down. He knows that when it's possible, he should move away from the offending garment. When it isn't possible, it's okay to try to cover his ears if he can.

In school, the paraprofessional assigned to Josh knows him well enough to head off a possible problem. The "scratchy" covers of the class agenda books make a noise that, to Joshua, is like fingernails on a blackboard. One year, Mrs. Gregus asked the class to cover their agenda books with smooth plastic or paper covers, and thankfully, almost all of them did.

School can be very stressful for our kids, but it's usually the less structured times, during recess, lunch or physical education, that incidents occur. After a while, it becomes a pattern, and the child with AS recognizes the pattern. In short order, he learns to dread the situation because of the difficulty in dealing with other children, unusual circumstances, and less supervision.

For Sharon Graebener's son Max, gym could be a stressful time, and one day, it was just too much.

"(Max) spit at the gym teacher," Sharon remembers. "I had to go in for a meeting with the gym teacher. Max was embarrassed at how he had expressed himself. I think the cafeteria smells got to him that day, he was overwhelmed, it was the afternoon, which is hard for him, and the gym teacher did something very innocently. He used Max as an example. He said, 'We're going to run like ponies,' and did a funny run, and said 'this is Max's run,' and Max thought he was making fun of him.

"(The teacher) wasn't making fun of him; he just used his name. He didn't know you don't do that with a child with autism spectrum disorder. Max started to scream, and when he did it again, Max spit. Max had to come with me to see the teacher, and he was humiliated. He did not want to go see him. I said, 'You have to apologize.' He apologized, but then turned to the man and said, 'You've ruined my life.' I said, 'No, Max, (the teacher) didn't ruin your life, you have to take responsibility for your actions, you did an impulsive act, and as long as you do not do it again, (he) will forgive you and you have to apologize. And you are allowed to leave. Next time something happens that upsets you, you should leave.' So I gave him an option, I told him what he should say next time. The teacher was shocked that I would be so firm with him. He said that to the aide the next day."

Many of our children have the option of leaving a classroom if the stress is too much for them to bear at any given moment. When he was in second grade, Josh left his gym class because he felt the teacher was picking on him. He meant to leave the school entirely, but the principal, alerted by the gym teacher, headed Josh off at the front door. It turned out the gym teacher was "picking on" Josh by insisting he tie his sneakers, which wasn't his best thing at the time. We got Josh a pair of Velcro sneakers, and things in gym were just fine again (it should be noted that he now ties his shoes quite well, and has done so for years).

Food issues, which many of our children have, can cause a good deal of anxiety in their minds. Knowing they are "picky" eaters leads children with AS to believe there will be problems when they go out to eat; certainly that was part of my son's anxiety. But there are other issues involved in eating with other people that can occasionally come into play.

"(Sean) eats anything; he just doesn't like to eat when people are watching him," says Ellen Silva. "We eat dinner at five 'o clock, Sean eats dinner at six 'o clock. You know what? As long as he's eating, it's OK. It drives other people crazy, but like I say, you choose your battles. We go out during off hours. On a Sunday, we'll skip lunch and go out to dinner at three 'o clock. The restaurants are less crowded, there's less chaos going on around him."

That's an accommodation, and one that works for everyone involved. Sean gets to eat without feeling like he's being watched, the family gets to go out to dinner without the threat of a tantrum and the restaurant doesn't have a meltdown during the dinner rush. As Ellen Silva says, "It drives other people crazy," and sometimes family members, for example, might find your accommodations to be strange or inconvenient. Your solution to the problem might not be the one that others would use. That doesn't matter. What works for you and your child – not to mention everyone else in your immediate family – is what you should do.

Difficult moments, however, don't only happen in restaurants. They can happen in school, at home, while shopping, at a friend's house – anywhere. Recognizing the problem ahead of time and planning to avoid or soften it can be the only defense. But be careful – sometimes, overcompensating for a problem can cause a larger problem.

"One o'clock is when the spiral starts (for Max)," says Sharon Graebener. "He's without his aide for forty-five minutes, alone with the teacher, who is very strict, and then goes into reading in the afternoon. (One of Max's teachers) said to me today, 'I know that Max occasionally needs to rage.' And I said, 'No, he doesn't.' In other words, she went to Autism 101 and learned that children with autism spectrum disorders rage. Well, children with high functioning autism will rage if you let them, sure, but no, he doesn't usually. She doesn't have a clue about autism. She's had Max for two months, and now it's ingrained in him that he goes in there and rages."

If you can't avoid the situation, and the worst happens (a meltdown), getting angry doesn't help. Believe me, I've tried it, and it doesn't help. What *should* you do?

Dealing with a full-blown Asperger tantrum in public is no fun, and it can't be ignored. And as any social worker, psychologist or law enforcement officer will tell you, there's no point in telling someone to "calm down." Instead, try to contain the situation. If you can, take the child to an area that's less public, like a rest room, a coatroom or a parking lot (even though it's outdoors, a parking lot is still removed from the situation and, presumably, the people immediately around it). Try to remain calm yourself (a statement often as useless as telling the child to calm down). Sympathize with the problem, but don't give in to unreasonable demands.

If, for example, your child is upset because the toy store at the mall doesn't have the exact model of Matchbox car he was anticipating, and he starts to bellow, you can try to head off the meltdown. You know the techniques that work best on your child: promise to try another store, ask the clerk when new shipments of Matchbox cars are coming in. If those don't work, and you've exhausted your repertoire, the tantrum is coming. You have to work fast.

See if there's a quiet corner where you can lead your child. Show him you're calm and unconcerned about the incident that has triggered this display, but tell him you're sorry the car he wanted isn't in stock.

Sometimes, distracting the child with a question can help. "What do *you* think we should do," you can ask. "Should we find another store that has Matchbox cars, or should we try to find one online when we get home?" This can get the child's mind working on the problem, which may stop the tantrum, and it will (hopefully) bring him closer to the conclusion that *this is a solvable problem*, something the child has probably not considered up to this point.

Of course, there are occasions when riding out the tantrum is the only feasible course of action. These are the most difficult times, and the solution to be used only when all else has failed. In this case, find the quietest spot possible, keep reassuring the child, and do anything that has worked in the past to calm him down. In your own mind, you can cling to the knowledge that in recorded history, no tantrum has lasted forever.

It is that kind of scene that leads many parents to avoid public excursions whenever possible. Sometimes, this accommodation is viable and reasonable. Other times, it can reign in a family's social life to the point of isolation, and that's unfair to all members of the family, not just the child with AS.

"I don't just hear it from parents of Asperger kids," says Dr. Baker. "I hear it from parents of any child who has challenging behaviors, whether they're on the autistic spectrum, or they're ADHD kids, or maybe very anxious youngsters who might throw tantrums if they happen to veer from what they're comfortable with. I hear it from every parent of kids who have challenging behaviors. They'd rather leave, or not go, than ride out a meltdown."

It's easy to give in to the impulse. It would be so much easier, sometimes, to avoid the situation, be sure there won't be a public scene, and stay away from the possible meltdown. And there are occasions when that is exactly the way to go – when the occasion is going to cause your child stress beyond the moment itself, or if he's not mature enough to handle it (keep in mind that our kids usually have a maturity level of about two-thirds their chronological age until very late in their teenage years), you should stay away. Even if all the other kids *have* seen that scary movie, your child might not be ready for it. Even if the whole family is going to be at the dinner party, eating at a formal table with a suit and tie on might be too much to ask of your child with AS.

You know best. If you think your child should be able to handle the situation, and you want to impress upon her the possibility that she can do things she didn't think she was capable of, prepare, prepare, prepare, and then give it your best shot.

"I have developed a saying that I repeat to Steven or he'll repeat to me when we're getting really frustrated with Adam," says Lori Shery. "And that is, 'It's hard being Adam.' That changes your perspective."

On the other hand, I must report that during one potential meltdown situation, I said to Josh, "It's not easy being you, is it?" It did diffuse the situation; Josh stopped, turned to me, and thought very hard for a moment. Then, he looked at me and said, "Why?"

Vacations with AS, and How to Survive Them

*M*ENTION THE WORD "VACATION" to the parent of a child with Asperger Syndrome, and you're likely to get one of two responses: a blank, uncomprehending stare, or a burst of laughter. Vacation, indeed.

To most of us, the idea of a vacation conjures up images of resorts, cities, activities and relaxation that are a welcome relief from the pressures of our lives the other fifty (or, in my case, 51.5) weeks of the year. We look forward to these breaks the way a marathon runner looks forward to the next water stop. We plan them meticulously in our minds, weigh options, fantasize about each possible adventure, and live in a state of heightened awareness for the time we're off, if only to savor each moment and store it away for recall when we're back in our "normal" lives. We don't necessarily live for our vacations, but our vacations certainly make it easier for us to live through the rest of the time.

To a child with Asperger Syndrome, a vacation is a terrifying break in the comfortable, safe routine that has been painstakingly established over years of effort. It is a time when everything is different, nothing feels right, all sorts of important events are missed (like television episodes, meals at a specific time, etc.) and the child's anxiety level rises above tolerable limits.

In other words, it is a recipe for disaster.

Going on vacation with a child who has AS is, as everything else involved with the disorder, a difficult process that requires more planning than it would for neurotypical people. Every aspect of every day has to be considered ahead of time, accommodations must be made for any number of contingencies and the child, especially, must be prepared well in advance for the disruption in his accustomed schedule.

For parents, it is like the stress of a dinner outing stretched out over a seven-day (or longer) period. It can be the exact antithesis of what a vacation is supposed to be.

Any parent – whether her children have autism spectrum issues or not – will tell you that long periods of time in a car with a child are not recommended. Add to that the adherence to routine and the devotion to ritual that can characterize AS, and you are headed for trouble.

On longer trips, any air traveler has a story about a flight that was made much more difficult by a child nearby crying, whining, unable to sit still, or complaining about the food or the movie. The stories are intensified by a factor of three any time the child in question has Asperger Syndrome.

Once at the destination, however, where parents of neurotypical children might be able to breathe a sigh of relief, the parents of children with AS are just warming up. Each meal will be a potential problem. Each day that goes by without the usual things happening in the usual order will be questioned. Thousands of dollars can be spent on activities, sightseeing and travel in which the child with AS may very well decline to participate. Imagine traveling all the way to Pisa and having your son refuse to view the Leaning Tower!

Then, once that is over, you have to go home.

If the above scenario is enough to put you off traveling, keep in mind that a vacation at home, with day trips planned, perhaps, is no guarantee for harmony and relaxation, either. If getting a child with AS out of the house once is a problem, imagine trying to do it every day for a week. Or twice a day. Think about the amount of planning that will have to go into finding something to do other than sit in the house, play video games and watch television. As a friend of mine once said about her ten-year-old son with AS, "The kid was born with 'frat house' written all over him."

Does vacation have to be this stressful with Asperger Syndrome along for the ride? Absolutely not. Parents who do enough planning ahead of time, take into account their children's personalities, and *don't set unrealistic expectations* can have a fine, relaxing time at home, or on a trip, even with their children with AS along.

Yes, it *can* be done.

"We vacation as a family frequently and it goes very well," reports Lori Shery. "We've been taking our kids on vacation since they were really little. We did the typical keep-them-busy stuff with the Gameboy and whatever in the car. Adam's special interest beyond religion is geography and travel. Every time we go places it's a thrill to him. We got lucky with that."

Not everyone can count on being so lucky, however. Kids with AS are no different than other children in some respects: long trips in the car are difficult for most children, probably until the age they start driving themselves. At least then, you don't have to tell them if you're there yet.

But there are ways to minimize the tedium. We have found book tapes from the library (preferably unabridged versions) are very helpful in holding Josh and Eve's attention when we're traveling even moderate distances. Various *Harry Potter* books have gotten us from New Jersey to Williamsburg, Virginia, and Binghamton, New York, among other, shorter trips. Sometimes, the kids don't want to get out of the car when we finally reach our destination because "the story's just getting good now."

Music tapes or CDs used to fill the bill, but a twelve-year-old boy and a nine-year-old girl rarely agree on *anything*, let alone taste in music. For those times, and for times when we might be traveling by air or train, we make sure each of our children has a personal stereo, so each can listen to the tunes that soothe the savage breast in peace. For a few minutes. Cassette stereos are very inexpensive, and CD players are not far behind. You can make your own tapes at home, or if you have a CD burner, create music mixes for each child.

Children who are not interested in music or recorded books might find the portable game system (that is, Gameboy) helpful. Electronic games can pass the time well for children who don't find looking down in the back seat a stomach-upsetting experience. It tends to get a touch pricey to keep up with the technology and the games that come out, but if your child isn't terribly worried about the trendiest thing on the market (and, luckily, children with AS are sometimes unaware of what the trendiest thing is), you can find used equipment and games at a discounted price.

Build extra time into the drive (if you're driving) for frequent stops. Food, bathrooms and just breathers are all necessary, and the child with Asperger Syndrome will probably need more than most, although some, who can immerse themselves in Gameboy or books, will likely want fewer interruptions. Some of the more upscale vans and SUVs now have video systems, as well, if you happen to have the funds to purchase them.

For those with food issues, it's important to bring the accepted snacks, since you can't count on highway rest stops, airport coffee shops or Amtrak club cars to stock exactly the right brand of potato chips or the right variety of apples. You're probably also bringing at least some packaged food for the vacation itself, but pack traveling food separately, where it's easy to get at.

All that, and you haven't arrived anywhere yet.

Even agreeing upon a destination that will be agreeable to all members of the family can be a trial. Children with AS who have a special interest might be adamant about visiting a spot that relates to the interest (the Decoy Museum in Maryland; Ben & Jerry's factory in Vermont; Warner Brothers Studios in Burbank, California). Strangely, the rest of the family might not find such destinations as fascinating. Some negotiation might be in order. Perhaps a trip to a destination near such areas, with a day trip to the desired haven included, is enough.

Many – but by no means all – children with AS will be placated with the usual theme parks and family-friendly resorts, but their vacation, and yours, will depend on a number of factors: your knowledge of your child and his limits; your expectations and their relation to reality; your ability to be flexible, since your child probably isn't, and everyone's capacity for patience with each other – something that seems to be in short supply for those who are trying, after all, just to relax.

"Every kid is different, and every kid with Asperger Syndrome is different," says Dr. Baker. "I (work with) some kids who refuse to do things: I'm not going there, I'm not going out. Once they get there, they're fine because they find they enjoy it. Anything new is scary because they haven't always been competent at things and they don't know what to expect. But then they enjoy it, so if you know that, it won't have to spoil your vacation. If this is the way your child is, you know once you're there, it'll be okay. You have other kids who are anxious about it ahead of time and they don't like it when they're there. They're unwilling to try something new. And that's harder. It's still an anxiety issue, so you can give some expectations to your youngster of what will happen, and then you might have to artificially pump up the rewards."

The reward system, within which the child is given a special reward for cooperating, for compromising when necessary, or for being patient, can be a very successful tactic to help a child with AS refocus from his anxiety over the vacation to something that will give him pleasure, the light at the end of the tunnel. Alas, I can't speak from experience with such things, since all our attempts to use a reward system for Josh have been unsuccessful. Josh has never met a reward under $50 that would entice him to cross from one side of the street to the other.

Still, parents for whom reward systems work will find them especially helpful in vacation situations. Remember, your child isn't seeing the break in routine the way you do: he thinks it's a horrible intrusion on his safe world, and that he'll be asked to do scary things that are outside his realm of experience. A reward can get him through each step of the way, and small rewards (for children who can be convinced to accept them) can be offered at regular steps along the way. If the carrot is always in sight, it's easier to focus on it.

Many parents use a reward system during their "regular life" and abandon it for vacations, but that doesn't seem to make much sense. Unless the child with AS is unusually flexible and able to accommodate to changes easily (which is not terribly consistent with the typical pattern of the disorder), vacation is the time of year when small rewards can be especially useful. Even Josh, for whom rewards do not work during the school year, can be encouraged with small rewards on a limited basis during vacations. The promise of stopping at his favorite highway restaurant for our lunch tomorrow can bring an agreement to come out with the family for dinner in an unfamiliar setting tonight.

Central to the concept of a pleasant family vacation with a child who has AS is the idea of *realistic expectations*. You can't expect that just because you are thrilled to be released from your workday routine, your child will be as elated. So expecting her to be thrilled with the idea of leaving home for a week to visit a huge, loud, crowded theme park (no matter how much money you know you spent on the trip) is probably not well grounded in reality.

"If you set your expectations a little lower for the vacation, if you imagine there are these things you want to do, and you plan that maybe your youngster can only do it for five minutes, but then he ends up being able to do it for half an hour, you'll be able to have a happier time," says Dr. Baker. "If you go in expecting that we're going to do this today, and then five minutes into it your youngster has a tantrum and won't go further, and you've paid your ticket already, you're not going to have such a good time. It's better if you set your expectations low. It may be even better if you can you take the vacation with the babysitter."

Not everyone can afford to bring a sitter along on vacation, but for those who can, and who employ one regularly during the year, this might be a welcome option. Even in "the happiest place on earth," a child or teen with AS might be happier staying in the hotel with a video game than experiencing the amazing sights, sounds and feelings of a theme park. Having someone along whose job it is to stay with your child while he does that, so the rest of the family *can* partake of the local atmosphere, might keep everyone happy. It's not a terribly logical way to the neurotypical world, but in the universe of AS, it can work.

Theme parks, too, have accommodations for children on the autism spectrum; in fact, it's one of the things they do best. Until recently, visitors to the Disney theme parks could avoid long lines, which tend to create scenes for children with AS, by obtaining a "handicapped" pass at the guest services desk upon entering. Families with such a pass, which is free, could enter even crowded attractions through separate entrances, bypassing long troublesome lines.

That accommodation, although still available, is not as necessary as it used to be, since many theme parks (including Disney's) are now offering reservations on their most popular attractions. Guests place a reservation for a specific ride or attraction, and are told at what time to return. The long, often hot, lines are once again avoided.

According to Dr. Baker, there are a number of ways to lower the stress of a vacation at a family-friendly attraction like Disney or Universal Studios, and the reservation system helps: "Now the Disney parks have a reservation system, so a lot of kids with disabilities don't need the extra help anymore. Again, taking help with you, so the youngster can sit in the hotel and work on the laptop while the other people go and do their travels, is an idea. Or offering (the child) incentives to participate and setting the expectations low, and maybe tag-teaming it – I'll go here, and you go there, and I'll stay with him or her."

For Ellen Silva, whose son Sean is now ten years old, taking a vacation with him and her teenaged daughter required a theme park, in order to give the two kids a common interest.

"Sean's into roller-coasters," she reports, and adds that her daughter shares the interest. "Especially having the difference of eight years between children, amusement parks are about the only thing they agree on. They both love the coasters. He will turn most conversations into roller coasters somehow or another."

Of course, not everyone wants to go to a theme park. Traveling to more exotic destinations, sightseeing and observing other cultures, is possible with a child who has AS. Like anything else, it requires more planning, much like we discussed above, but it can be done. Maggie Casciato, whose son Tom is twenty-two years old, went on a family vacation with her husband, Tom and his brother, and found that traveling was actually easier than staying at home. The two young men, who do not get along at home, had no choice but to do so abroad.

"Last year, we took them to London, and they had to share a bedroom, because we weren't going to have separate rooms," she recalls. "For a week, they tolerated each other and actually had a decent time. Prior to that, we didn't even bother trying to have family vacations, because we knew it would just be the two of them fighting. When they were little, we couldn't afford it, and when they were older and we could afford it, we didn't want the grief."

For foreign travel, parents who give their children medication should be careful to have it at hand when going through customs, to speed things along. Also, make sure there is an adequate supply of medication to last the vacation, since getting a prescription anywhere away from home can be very difficult.

Making sure there is at least one point of particular interest to the child with AS is essential in less family-themed travel. Tours of ruins and museums may be fascinating to the other members of the family, but if the child with AS doesn't see something of interest to him – let's say, the ruins of Pompeii for a child with a special interest in volcanoes – the trip could be very uncomfortable for everyone.

My son Josh is a very good traveler, but we haven't stretched his boundaries beyond what we know he will accept. A trip to France, for example, would be difficult, given Josh's food issues. A vacation in Disney World is just about his favorite thing, but we've also visited Williamsburg, Vermont, Washington, DC, and other areas within driving distance of our home, and Josh has enjoyed each trip. Of course, we plan ahead, but we plan ahead for a trip to the supermarket, so we've gotten into the habit.

For Lori Shery, traveling with her son Adam has always been a pleasure. On the other hand, her younger son Zachary, who is neurotypical, has not always been so cooperative. "He was my tough one when we went on vacation when he was little," Lori says of Zachary. "We used to take family vacation pictures, and it was always Steve and me and Adam. Zachary always had an attitude. We have what we call our stinkpot pictures. We have Steven and me and Adam in front of the Jefferson Memorial and then we have a picture of Zachary on a far-off hill standing with his hands on his hips. He was asserting his authority, and wasn't going to listen. It's always been easy with Adam, and as Zachary matured and became a *mensch*, he's been wonderful, too."

See? It *can* be done.

So Sue Me: Sometimes AS Is Funny

*I*T'S MY FAVORITE ASPERGER SYNDROME story, and it happened when Josh was about six years old.

It was winter, and cold, and he was wearing his heavy coat and boots when he stomped in the front door after school one day. Josh was clearly in the middle of an AS meltdown that had been triggered at school, something that might have happened when he was in class (this was before he had a paraprofessional with him) or outside the building on the way home. Whatever it was, it was eating at him.

He decided he'd take it out on his father, since I was the one who greeted him at the front door. Josh stomped into the house, threw his book bag on the floor, and yelled at me that he had had a bad day. He called me names. He tromped in and out of rooms. He muttered to himself. Finally, he sat in a heap just to the left of my desk, grumbling and flapping his hands.

Through it all, I was uncharacteristically calm. For some reason, this particular display wasn't affecting me; I sat watching, not reacting at all. When he sat down near my desk, I stole a glance in his direction. I remember word-for-word what I said.

"It's none of my business, Josh," I told him, "but why don't you at least take that heavy coat off?"

That was it. Josh leapt to his feet, fuming Asperger ire with every breath. He ripped the coat off and threw it to the floor, glaring at me the whole time.

"You make me do *everything* around here!" he screamed, and stomped off to his room.

I didn't even mention the boots.

You can disagree with me all you like, but I think there are times when Asperger Syndrome is funny. Sure, another boy might have said the same thing at the same time, but he wouldn't have put quite the same *oomph* into it. Another six-year-old could have forgotten to take off his coat, but he probably would have noticed how warm it was in the room. After a few minutes, anyway. A neurotypical child might very well have gotten angry with his father, but would have chosen his words differently.

In the beginning, when Josh didn't yet have his diagnosis and we were shuttling back and forth to psychologists, behaviorists and psychiatrists looking for a solution, my wife and I would inevitably make the same statement to the doctor: we just want to understand what's happening. We want to help him. We don't want Josh to stop being Josh.

Are there times when I wish my son was neurotypical? Sure there are; if only because it would mean an easier life for *him*. But are there just as many times, maybe more, when I marvel at the wonder that he is, when I stand in awe of his mind, his creativity, his infinite potential? You'd better believe there are. And sometimes, as a parent, you have to take a step back, observe the situation, and if you're lucky, let out a laugh. It's not all misery.

Plenty of times when my wife and I are with Josh at a fast food restaurant, a store or a movie theatre, we observe the other families. We'll shake our heads at the same things – children walking without flapping their arms, visibly paying attention to the things their parents say, sitting quietly in strollers – and one of us will look at the other and ask, "How can the parents of the 'normal' kids stand it? They must be so *bored!*"

Asperger Syndrome can make a child many things, but to a parent, the word you hear most often in discussion is "interesting."

When Josh was about eight, we attended a party at my cousin's home. Some of the adults were playing an electronic game similar to tic-tac-toe, but with four squares in each row rather than three. Josh observed, then asked if he could play. After a few minutes, he was regularly beating the adults without seeming to try very hard.

One of the guests, a young man about twenty or so, walked over to me while this was going on. He told me that he had been in statewide chess competitions, and that we should encourage Josh to take up the game, as the type of anticipation and strategy that went on in the game he was playing could indicate advanced chess aptitude. So when we got home that night, I took out the chessboard and gave Josh a quick lesson in the basics of chess – how the pieces move, what the ultimate goal is.

Within a week, he could beat me whenever he wanted to. Now, given that I'm no chess master, this wasn't a really strong test of his skill, but it was something. My wife suggested we get Josh to a local chess teacher, who was offering lessons in his home.

When I suggested this to Josh, he looked at me with the most puzzled expression I'd ever seen. "Why do I need lessons?" he asked. "I *know* how to play chess."

To Josh, with his AS perspective, knowing which pieces move where and what you're trying to accomplish is enough. He is not interested in process; he wants results. We could have forced him to go for chess lessons, but it would have been a futile gesture. Why bother teaching the boy to play a game he'd already decided he knew how to play?

If there is nothing else you remember, nothing else you take away from reading this book, remember this: *a sense of humor is absolutely essential to keeping your sanity while you raise a child with Asperger Syndrome.* Absolutely essential. Because this disorder is designed specifically to push every parental hot button, approaching it without an eye for the absurd is like diving into a shark pool without a protective cage. You're asking to be eaten alive.

There is another consideration to be made: our children, although they do have a disorder that will make their lives more complicated than most, are not at severe health risk. They can be taught to lead the best possible lives they can lead. Yes, there will be challenges, there will be differences. But there will be lives, as well. It may be a negative human characteristic, but it is present in each of us: it's comforting to look at someone whose lot in life is more difficult than yours and say, "Maybe I'm not so bad off, after all."

Maggie Casciato recalls a time before her son Tom was diagnosed with an autism spectrum disorder, when she didn't have a name for his behaviors. But he had a special interest in electrical and mechanical devices, which were his favorite playthings.

"I still remember when he was in nursery school: each nursery school teacher makes a visit to the child's house once a year, to get to know the kid a little more and see what they're interested in," Maggie remembers. "Tom was all excited that his teacher was coming to the house, and lined up his favorite things all along the floor for her to see. He had the toaster, and the blender, and the juicer … I thought, 'something is not normal here.'"

Because we see the humor in a situation does *not* mean we are making fun of our children's disorder. That is absolutely not the case. Josh will often say something, then look at me and shake his head, as if he's just heard his own thought for the first time and wondering how such a thing could pop into his head. He knows he's not the same as other children, and sometimes that works to his advantage.

Many of our children are extremely bright, and Josh is no exception. A number of years ago, for example, when we told him about AS, and what it meant (although I'm still not one hundred percent sure he understands it completely), I explained to him that his brain was perfectly healthy, but that it operated a little differently than most others.

A few weeks later, he came home with an unusually large amount of homework, and was upset by that. Grumbling, he watched as I read the note from his aide, detailing what needed to be done. When I was done, he looked expectantly at me.

"Well?" he said.

"Well, what?"

"How much of this homework do I have to do?" Josh asked.

I raised my eyebrows. "All of it, of course," I told him.

Josh's frustration practically sprang out of his eyes. "But I *can't*," he lamented. "My brain is *different!*"

Nice try, Josh.

Because the children with AS are usually bright, and because they can notice that they have differences, they sometimes overcompensate for their differences, which doesn't usually have the desired effect of making them seem more "normal." But even that can be used to an advantage if the child and the parent have a sense of humor.

"(Sean's teacher) told me they were coming in from a code white drill, which is evacuating the school," recalls Ellen Silva. "She teasingly calls him her megadroid. One of the other teachers heard her say that and commented about it. (Sean's teacher) can't remember what it (the other teacher said), but it rhymed with Detroit. Sean repeated the comment on the way into school to the principal. Whatever it was, it was funny, because he giggled. The principal said to the teacher, 'I don't understand this. He's the most well adjusted child in this school.'"

Having a sense of humor about AS isn't limited to our children, by any means. Parents who can laugh at themselves have an enormous advantage, and will probably get through life ulcer-free. Lori Shery remembers a time very early on, before she realized her son Adam was on the spectrum.

"(My husband) Steven and I saw the movie *Rain Man* when Adam probably was two or three years old. We sat there and said, 'Adam does that,' but it never occurred to us that he might have a form of autism, because autism to me meant being severely impaired and unintelligent. So to me it was just a coincidence that Dustin Hoffman's character was doing it." Lori says this with a chuckle today.

Often, parents find themselves in situations that don't start out funny, but end up in another area. When Josh was about three, my wife was making him a piece of cinnamon toast, and she and I were discussing something. When I turned around, Josh had taken the container of cinnamon and sugar, and walked over to where our dog was eating from her dish. He was quite methodically pouring the cinnamon onto the white dog, causing her to take on an orange hue.

My first reaction, of course, was to stop him, and take the bottle out of his hands. "Josh!" I shouted. "Don't cinnamon the dog!"

Sometimes, you have to turn away so the child doesn't see you laughing.

The times when our children generally are not funny, naturally, is when they think they're being funny. One mother I know has a son, age eleven, whose special interest is in 1940s pop culture: cartoons, radio programs on cassette, and movies. His speech is often inflected with idioms from the period, making him sound like a Humphrey Bogart movie played at 78 rpm.

When we visited his family once, this boy had gotten small gifts for everyone in my family, which was a very sweet gesture on his part. I walked over to thank him for my present, and put my hand on his shoulder.

"Thanks for the gift," I said. "It was really nice of you."

"I know," said the boy. "Ain't I a riot?"

Humor is not a simple concept, and it's not one that all children on the autism spectrum can grasp. Josh has a terrific sense of humor, but it's more an appreciative thing. He has a hard time telling jokes, and the awful puns he thinks are amusing usually cause groans in everyone else.

He does, however, write poetry, and some of it is very funny. His companion pieces, "My Mother Is a Monster" and "My Father Is a Fish" have become favorites in his school, and he has been asked to read them at assemblies more than once. Everyone has a particular outlet for humor, and in order to be a successful Asperger parent, you need to find yours. You don't have to become Groucho Marx and you don't have to bone up on joke books, but you do need to recognize the humor in a situation, even one that on its surface might seem like the kind of thing that would cause Hans Asperger himself to pull his hair out.

When your child barges into the house after school complaining because the cafeteria has switched to a new brand of salt and he just can't eat it, you can cringe and gnash your teeth, or you can chuckle and explain why maybe that isn't the most important thing that happened today. When you tease your daughter playfully and then explain that you were just "pulling her leg," you can cry or laugh when she looks at her leg, then back at you, in wonder. The choice of reaction is yours.

Lori Shery finds humor in the way her son Adam can take things a bit too literally, and she offers a scenario that she says hasn't happened, but certainly could: "If I said to Adam, 'Put the dog outside and then brush your hair,' the next thing I know I would see him brushing her hair with his brush," she says. "I always hear that from him, 'You weren't specific enough.' 'You didn't tell me not to do that.' They're really adorable and delicious, and they're really interesting. We have really interesting kids. It sounds cliché, but I think that having a child with special needs for many, if not most, makes us better human beings."

Maybe it does. Bringing up a child with AS can bring out the best or the worst in a parent, but most of us find the experience to be a positive one. With the right perspective, we can find something every day that at least adds a smile, and that's never a bad thing. Josh always manages to do something in the course of a day that makes me glad to be his father. Maybe parents of neurotypical children feel that on a daily basis, too, but they might not notice it quite as deeply.

The fact of the matter is, we can cry about our children's disorder, or we can see the beauty of it, the gift it can be (on occasion). A large part of that gift is the humor that can be found in a child with Asperger Syndrome, and I don't think it's a bad thing to acknowledge it. In fact, I think it would be a crime to let it go unnoticed. Don't bury the funny parts of the day in the backyard; cherish them and retell them to yourself periodically so they won't be forgotten. They are the most important things you will ever own, your happier memories.

This will be the last example, I promise:

The other day, Josh came home after a full day of school and immediately launched into his homework. That done, he went into the kitchen to find himself a snack, and sat down at the table to eat it. I just happened to be looking at the clock in my office when I heard a sigh from the kitchen; it was ten minutes after four in the afternoon. I walked in to see what was wrong, and nothing appeared to be amiss. Josh was sitting at the table, eating his snack. He sighed again, clearly wanting to attract my attention.

"What's the matter, Josh?" I asked.

His voice was a lament. "Oh, nothing," he said. "I just noticed that my shirt has been on backwards all day." He paused for a moment, then went back to his eating.

Don't ask me to cry over that.

Fear Factor

$\mathcal{F}$OR MOST OF US, THE FIRST TIME WE heard the words "Asperger Syndrome" was when our children were being diagnosed. So we weren't just hearing about a disorder we'd never encountered before, we were being told our children had it.

There are myriad emotions we feel at a time like that: worry, disappointment, sadness, in some cases relief (that it isn't something worse), anger, concern. But the one word that pops up most often when parents talk about their emotions is *fear*.

We're all afraid of something related to our children's AS, and it's not always the same thing. Some of our fears are entirely rational and based on the scientific data being gathered about Asperger Syndrome, and others will not stand up to logical scrutiny. But they are no less real.

For example: I know, from having read about autism spectrum disorders and literature on AS, that our children, from the

time they are about nine years old until they are eighteen, oper-
ate on an emotional level that is roughly two-thirds of their
chronological age. Josh, at twelve, acts like an eight- or nine-
year-old. I also know that this aspect of the disorder will
improve; by the time Josh is twenty-four, for example, his emotional age should be indistinguishable from any other man in his
mid-20s. I know that because there is scientific proof, literature
by clinicians who have performed painstaking studies and for-
mulated conclusions over years of research. I know it because it
is a proven scientific fact.

I just don't believe it, that's all.

My deepest fear for Joshua right now is that he will
"plateau" emotionally, that he will always be someone who acts
like a child. He still cries too easily, uses phrases that are inappropriate for his age, has a higher-than-average voice, and in all
manner except physically, could be mistaken for a much
younger child. You can tell me from today until the end of next
week that AS isn't that kind of condition, that no one with AS
has ever exhibited this problem, that every single child with AS
manages his or her way through adolescence and eventually
finds emotional maturity. Even though the intellectual part of
my brain will agree with you, the emotional side is from
Missouri, and must be shown something before it will believe
you. When I can talk to my son and conduct a conversation on
the same level as his chronological age, I will be convinced.
Until then, it's all theory.

There's no point in talking about being an Asperger parent
without discussing fear. It's not something any of us wants
to confront, but it exists in our minds, and it can cloud our
judgment and influence the choices we make for our children.
In some cases, it must be noted, our fears are absolutely well
founded, and should be respected. Other examples, like my concerns about Josh hitting an emotional "plateau," are not rational,
and must be flushed out and examined so we can better ignore
them when we're making choices.

For some of us, depending on how severely our children are affected, the fears center on the future: how will our children react when it's time to enter school, transition to high school, go away to college, enter the workforce? Will they be able to form close enough interpersonal relationships to marry and have families of their own? Will they be self-sufficient enough to live on their own when they're adults? What will happen to them after we're gone?

These are all legitimate concerns, and this is not the place to address them individually. But they do cause parents to lose sleep, to down antacids and to consult therapists. It's important to admit to our fears, to confront them, and to deal with them in some way, even if they can't be resolved. Fear is part of all parenting (everybody worries about their children), but for Asperger parents, the fears are more direct, more concrete, and in some cases, more serious.

Sharon Graebener's son Max literally rolled into one of her greatest fears when he was roller blading with his father: "They are going down a street where they constantly go roller blading and the road itself was being repaired, but they went on the sidewalk," she says. Unfortunately, the sidewalk was also being repaired, and the concrete was fresh. The owner of the home was upset, and called the police, and that is what Sharon is most concerned about. As it turned out, the incident was handled without further difficulty, but Sharon's psyche was already scarred.

She says, "I told my husband the other day when Max was not having a good day, 'You know, I can't take the police in ten years. I cannot go through that.' That's why I think it's so important to get our kids understanding that they have to control their behavior. All these kids are going to be out there. It scared me when that happened with the police."

For Sharon, fear of involvement with the legal system is a driving motive. "You see the young man from Columbine," she says of the high school students who shot their classmates and their teachers. "I think about the young man who went to the

Capitol building and shot the security officer. He had schizophre-
nia and it didn't show up until he was eighteen or nineteen. His
parents were clueless."

For many of us, the idea of our children becoming entangled
with the criminal justice system, either through their own misun-
derstanding of the system, or the system's inability to recognize
and accommodate autism spectrum disorders, is enough to keep
us awake nights. Our children, when they are older especially, do
not appear to be "different" physically, but do not respond to
social situations (particularly stressful ones) in the same way as
neurotypically developing people. Law enforcement officers often
carry guns, and the combination can be very, very disturbing.

Public Advocate

Dennis Debbaudt is a licensed private investigator and an
advocate for people on the autism spectrum, like his teenage son
Kelly. He is also the author of *Autism, Advocates and Law
Enforcement Professionals: Recognizing and Reducing Risk Situations
for People with Autism Spectrum Disorders* (Jessica Kingsley Pub.,
2001). He has seen encounters between the police and people
with autism from both sides, and he feels that a good deal of education must be done, and now.

"If you're on the spectrum, you're more likely to inadver-
tently come under suspicion by the police," Dennis says. "If you
have the condition, you will display behaviors and characteristics
that others who don't know you have the conditions will find suspicious." This leads to people who don't understand AS calling
the police because someone on the street is "acting suspiciously."
And encounters between people with AS and the law enforcement system result.

"The problem is that these kids or adults are found to be
suspicious by other people, quite naturally," says Dennis. "I think
mid-functioning people are most at risk, because they have the
independent skills to be in the community alone and seek to do

that. But out there their decision making is so spotty that they may make misjudgments or bad decisions. They may be more susceptible to suggestions from others. I think that's certainly the case. That can really put them at risk out there."

Because the level of social skills in people with AS is lower than average, young people and adults with autism spectrum disorders often find themselves more susceptible to suggestions from "friends" than others. For example, it is not unusual for young adults to become involved in activities they wouldn't normally contemplate because associates or people they know coerce them into action.

"I reported in my book on a fellow up in Pittsburgh who was caught. He had a lot of knowledge about computers, had a beautiful computer, a beautiful printer attached, and was a whiz at it, which many people on this spectrum are," Dennis recalls. "His so-called friends, recognizing that skill, convinced to him to make some bad paper (counterfeit money). And he was caught at it. He was making fifties and hundreds. The whole ring got caught. He was doing it to keep his friends. His friends were just saying, 'do this,' and he did it to keep the friends."

By the same token, there was a young man in England whose friends talked him into another type of difficulty. Dennis says: (he) "worked in a jewelry store and was convinced by his friends to bring samples home. And he did, of course, and got into a lot of trouble. In order to keep the friends, they do things like that, and that same mindset goes into if they're being quizzed by the police and interrogated, they will fall prey to the friendly cop routine. In order to keep a friend, I'll say anything I need to. It all comes back to bad judgment and lack of common sense."

These stories are not included here to keep you awake at night. The vast majority of our children are not criminals, and will not be coerced into criminal acts. But a lack of training on our part, a lack of advocacy in general for spectrum disorders, and a lack of education on the part of the criminal justice system can combine to make it seven times more likely a person with AS will have an encounter with the police than a neurotypical person of the same age. According to Dennis Debbaudt, it's not time to focus on the problem; it's time to concentrate on how to prevent future problems from occurring.

"We're doing it," he says. "It can be done through local advocates. There are people all over the world now who are forming partnerships with their local law enforcement agencies, which train the law enforcers or certify them to work in local areas. Wherever you go in the U.S. you will find they have their own police academy. Usually the recruits go to the Academy and then come into their own department and are given specific training there. That's where we ultimately want to get this information. The only way we're going to get there is to convince our local law enforcers that it's not only useful, but the wave of the future. They haven't considered this. And they're not going to consider it unless we tell them about it. If the community stays mute, they're not going to know about it. Bad things happen reactively. We, the autism spectrum community, need to be proactive in identifying our needs to the law enforcement community. I always hear, 'they (the police) should have known that.' My answer to that is, 'Why? Why should they have known that?' They're not swamis out there. We need to have a better effort within the autism community. Ultimately we need to educate the judges, the prosecutors, the law enforcement community."

In a post-9/11 world, tolerance is at a new low, and for understandable reasons. It was, naturally, a week after the World Trade Center towers fell that my son decided, in a fit of pique over having to work in groups during his social studies class, to announce that he wanted to burn down his school. (I recall mentioning that Josh has a talent for finding the least socially acceptable response to any situation.)

The teacher, who didn't know Josh very well (it was the second full week of the school term), reported the incident to the principal, since the remark was made in the presence of other students, whom the teacher felt might become upset, given the climate in the New York/New Jersey area at that time. The principal, who was in the first month of her tenure, talked to me, then was obligated to refer the matter to the school psychologist.

Luckily, the school psychologist knew Josh well (and had been his case manager for two years previous to this incident). She, Josh and I met in the school one morning, and after emphasizing to Josh exactly how serious his statement was, particularly in the shadow of the terrorist attacks, and that he could end up getting involved with the police, she turned to me.

"Once I saw who it was," she said, pointing to the report, "I knew there was no problem."

I knew we had dodged a bullet, but my school system has been very understanding and helpful with Josh since he entered kindergarten. Some other systems are not as cooperative. You can't count on the reaction being the same as the one I encountered, and still, both Josh and his parents were shaken pretty seriously after that episode.

Dennis Debbaudt: "I'm working with families around the world whose AS loved ones, some as young as ten years old, get into trouble with tantruming and outbursts, physical confrontations. The verbal outbursts, the verbal terroristic acts, that's how the law looks at that. You or I don't have any excuse if we say we're going to do that. That's a felony. It's a terroristic threat. Technically, they could charge a kid with doing that."

"Some families are reporting to me, and this is anecdotal, some school districts are waiting for or encouraging this kind of activity so they can get these kids out of school," he continues. "(The schools) don't want to deal with the (students). This is not a good prospect; it's absolutely awful. Either the terroristic verbal threat or the retaliatory physical confrontation is precipitated by bullying, harassments or teasing. If that goes unchecked ... our kids will react. It's highly predictable that they will be teased, bullied and harassed. The problem is that often it is the retaliator who is caught."

For young adults or adults with AS, the issues become more serious. Those seeking companionship, or attention from the opposite sex, can be misconstrued because they don't always know the proper social cues. People who can't read body language or tone of voice might not understand the power of "no" when it isn't said directly. And if the person with AS persists, legal problems can ensue.

"Stalking can be physical, it can be over the phone or on the Internet. Those are areas that people on the high-functioning end are getting into trouble with," Dennis says. "I think that they are seeking friendship or perhaps a mate, and they don't have the social skills to know when to quit. Someone says hello to them and they automatically believe that's a friend, somebody that you could just go visit. Or they may become argumentative and not understand. They may have felt slighted, rightly or wrongly, and lack the social skills to appropriately let someone else know that they're upset. So it turns into, 'I'll call them up and hang up all the time. I'll punish them and get my revenge.'"

But even that isn't as complicated as it can get. Social skills are inherent in sexual relationships, too, and as people with AS go through adolescence and young adulthood, they are just as interested in intimacy as anyone else, but less well equipped to deal with it.

"Inappropriate sexual contact is possible, too," Dennis says. "It could be inadvert; it could be that they have the intent. Because I write about being proactive about this issue, and because I am proactive and have a receptive audience, all of the problem cases (I am called in on) are reactive. It used to be one or two a month. Now it's getting to be two or three a day. 'My kid got caught, what do I do? We need to react; we need to react.' You don't need to call me; you know how to react."

Dennis realizes that some parents believe his work paints children and adults with AS as more likely than others to commit crimes and get into difficult situations with law enforcement. He says that view is inaccurate, that his work is meant to help prevent our children from being misunderstood and make their lives happier and easier.

"Some parents look at this issue, and without hearing what I have to say, think this makes their kids look like criminals," he says. "Others are not prepared yet to think about the future. Probably the best way I get through that is to ask, 'What do you do when you get in the car every morning? You put this seat belt on, right?' Many of us have life insurance policies. Most people in the country lock the front door and the back door before they go to bed at night. Does everybody freak out when they do that? Do you shudder in fear when you put the seat belts on? When you write the checks for the insurance policy, does that freak you out? And 99.9% of the time, nothing happens. You do these things. It's just a precaution in everyday life."

Dennis does see the possibility of solutions. Chief among these is education, both for families on the spectrum and for law enforcement personnel. Debbaudt and other advocates are beginning that process. With his knowledge of the criminal justice system, Debbaudt believes he is seen as more credible by the law enforcement agencies he lectures, and because he is the parent of a child with AS, he knows the issues that face a person on the autism spectrum.

"If somebody (calls) 9-1-1, and (police or emergency personnel) show up on the scene, we have to give them enough information so that they can make a judgment that this person has autism or Asperger Syndrome," says Debbaudt. "The feedback I get from the cops is, 'Yeah, if somebody had given me a card that says autism or Asperger Syndrome now, after going to a workshop, I'd know how to respond.' It becomes a general safety issue when someone presses 9-1-1. If someone from the general public sees my son and he's talking to himself, and he standing outside a bank or a 7-Eleven, they press 9-1-1. (Police officers) are called to the suspicious person in front of a bank. If they go up to my kid and he is still doing that routine, if they don't know any better, the next thing you know they're restraining him and soon they have him on the ground. Getting through to them on key, basic issues, the first-response issues, even the detective bureau issues like the false confession and victim witness statements, and how to get better at that, they're very responsive to that, and that's the first line of this (education program)."

That's just part of the program. It's just as essential that children with AS be taught the proper responses to give law enforcement personnel, and ways to avoid being caught in the wrong situations to begin with. To Dennis, this type of information has been sadly lacking in the special training our children have been getting.

"What haven't we done?" he asks. "We haven't given our kids enough education on how to recognize and respond well to the police. Can educators start delivering that message a little better? Sure. If parents cooperate and agree that's a good issue, that can easily be done."

He also emphasizes that children need to know exactly how serious it can be to react the wrong way in these situations, and believes that parents who shield their children from the harsh realities of the outside world are doing them a disservice. Debbaudt says he never avoided the more unpleasant realities in talking to his son, who was diagnosed with AS at age four:

"We told him right away. We never hid it around our house. He'd hit out at people or push other kids. We taught him early and often – and we still reinforce it – that Kelly, you can't hit other people, you can't touch other people, you can't destroy property and you can't say you're going to do it, either. He's asked, 'what will happen if I do' and I'll say, 'you'll go to jail.' Don't pull any punches with these kids. You've got to tell them."

If it sounds like a grim world, that's because it can be. But that doesn't mean it has to be. Our deepest fear might be that of our children becoming involved with the police, but if we strive to educate the police to autism spectrum disorders, and if we educate our children and school system personnel, we can avoid many of the situations Dennis Debbaudt sees every day.

No, it's not a pretty picture. But it is one that we can repaint more to our taste.

To Medicate, Or Not to Medicate

RITALIN.

There. I said it. My son Joshua has been taking Ritalin for most of his life, from the time he was a little less than six until today. He takes 15 mg in the morning and another 10 mg just about noon, when he makes a trip to the school nurse for "meds." If you want to argue with me about that, I'm sure the publisher of this book would be happy to forward your letter to me. I'm not sure I'll answer, but that's another story.

Medication is possibly the most divisive, most hotly debated, most contentious, most discussed issue among parents of children on the autism spectrum. People who normally have civil, even friendly, empathetic conversations about the trials and travails of their children with Asperger Syndrome can come within an eyelash of a fistfight if they disagree on the issue of medication: to give it or not to give it. That is the question.

Don't look for the answer here. The decision to give a child medication, or not, how much and what kind, should never be sought in books, particularly those written by people who have had absolutely no medical training. That decision is to be made by the child's parents and his/her doctor. Any other advice is superfluous, and can be harmful. Each child is different, each parent has personal views on the subject, and each doctor will explain and advise differently. You know your child. I, in all likelihood, have never met your child. Don't ask me if you should give him medication.

I know Asperger parents who, like me, have felt that some medications can help their children through the day and do no harm. Others believe in some medicines and not others. There is a large group who believe that medicating children for AS is a search for a "quick fix," and they reject the idea. Some believe in dietary changes, eliminating dairy or wheat from the child's diet entirely. They swear by it. If I tried that with Joshua, he might exhibit fewer AS behaviors, but he'd more than likely starve to death (his diet is based on wheat and dairy products), and that would be a serious downside.

The point is, none of these philosophies is to be endorsed or rejected for every child with Asperger Syndrome. It would be like saying that every person on the planet should drive a Buick. While that plan might be very popular at General Motors, it would fail to take into account the vast diversity of needs and tastes in the overwhelming majority of people on the planet.

By the same token, saying that every child with AS would benefit from Ritalin would be naïve and ill conceived. For Josh, the drug has proven to help him concentrate on schoolwork during the day and, to a certain extent, helps him control his emotional reaction to situations that crop up in the course of the average school day. He has not increased his dosage drastically since he started taking Ritalin in 1996, but the effect it has is noticeable, even while it may not be dramatic.

Of course, that is an anecdotal report on one child taking one drug over the course of six years. It has no bearing on anyone else's child, and may no longer be relevant for Josh in a year or two. There is no reason to believe that the results my son achieves with medication will be duplicated with your child. We can't even be absolutely sure that Josh wouldn't have reaped the same benefits over the past six years without Ritalin. But I've seen him on the weekends, when we generally don't bother giving him a pill, and I'm willing to go on the record as saying I think it makes him a more confident, more even-keeled, easier person to live with.

Some parents feel that giving a child with AS any medication whatsoever is a mistake, that autism spectrum disorders should be confronted with alternate teaching methods and education of the general public. I agree that we should have alternatives in teaching and learning, and wholeheartedly agree that the neurotypical public must better understand AS, but I have not seen Ritalin do my son any harm.

"One of my mantras is, 'a trial is just a trial.' You can just try it," says Dr. Elizabeth Roberts, the pediatric neuropsychologist. "(Some parents) think the kid's going to get addicted to it, that he'll be on medication until he's ninety-six if he starts today."

It was difficult for us to start Josh on the medication, because we were not interested in changing his personality; we wanted him to be Josh. But the pediatric neurologist who first prescribed Ritalin for him explained a few facts: the drug would *not* alter Josh's personality, but it would help him control himself and pay attention better. Because Ritalin was seen as a stimulant, the illegal drug of choice on college campuses for those who needed to pull an all-nighter before a big exam, it seemed that we were giving our son exactly what he didn't need: a more hyper nature.

Not at all. The neurologist explained that for those who *need* it, Ritalin provides the kind of sensory stimulation that people like Josh feel is lacking, the reason they are often uncomfortable in everyday situations. With the extra stimulation, Josh feels more typical, not less, and will therefore behave less jittery, not more. We had noticed that when his pediatrician had prescribed a particular decongestant for Josh's ear infections, and warned us that "this one tends to make them hyper," the pill would put Joshua to sleep.

The most comforting thing our neurologist said, however, was that even if Ritalin was not something that would help Josh in the slightest, it would be out of his system in a few hours, and no remnants of the drug would remain. It felt like it was worth a try.

She also warned us that Ritalin isn't supposed to work with children who have AS, but that Josh exhibited some signs of ADD as well, and that might be positively affected by the drug. He started taking it, his behavior seemed more consistent, and above all, he seemed happier. We have continued the medication.

Of course, like everyone else involved in the autism spectrum, we had read studies that suggested Ritalin could inhibit the child's appetite, and therefore cause him not to grow at the normal rate, so Josh is measured in his doctor's office every four months as a part of his Ritalin therapy. He is about two inches shorter than I am right now, which is not a great feat (I'm pretty short), but one has to keep in mind that he is twelve years old, and I'm forty-four. His growth is exactly right on the doctor's charts. And I look forward to the day, not long from now, when I will have to look up into his face.

Again, I am not trying to tell you that Ritalin is the answer, or even *an* answer, for your child. I'm merely saying that it seems to have done my child some good. If I sound a bit defensive about it, that comes from years of experience.

Other parents – even parents of other children on the autism spectrum – feel it is their right, in fact their *duty*, to inform my wife and me that we are unnecessarily medicating our son. This comes from a genuine concern, and we appreciate that, but I would never consider telling another parent he or she was doing harm to a child unless I saw evidence of criminal abuse. Even while writing a book that is meant to advise parents of children with AS, I feel it is necessary to say that this is simply advice, I don't know your child, and you are the person who has the ultimate responsibility, so don't listen to me unless what I say makes sense to you. I wouldn't dream of telling you how to raise your child.

In the meantime, don't tell me how to raise mine, either.

A friend of ours, whose child was diagnosed with AS a year or so after Josh, once asked me why we gave our son Ritalin. Thinking she wanted to know about Ritalin versus another medication, I outlined why the neurologist had prescribed it, and how we'd come to the decision that a trial period was worthwhile. My friend took a moment and looked at me when I finished speaking.

"But don't you feel," she said, "like you should try other things? A change in diet? Something short of mood-altering drugs?"

I knew she had experienced some success with her son by changing his diet, but her son was, I felt it necessary to point out, *not* my son, and Ritalin was not a mood-altering drug. Josh's diet was so limited to begin with that adding chocolate pudding would be a major event. Taking gluten or dairy away from him would require months of painstaking, hideous coercion and ugly scenes of family dinners gone to hell. Should we take steps to change Josh's diet? Sure, we should. Is it a fight I'm willing to take on right now? Um … I'll get back to you on that.

The point was that even another Asperger parent feels comfortable challenging our position on giving our child medication which: (a) was prescribed by his physician; (b) can be eliminated from his system entirely in a matter of a few hours; and (c) has done him absolutely no measurable harm.

I finally determined that medication, like politics or religion, was a subject best left out of most friendly conversations.

The other stumbling block for parents whose children might benefit from medication is that sometimes (as in Josh's case) the child will need to take some of that medication during the school day, so the child will have to leave class (or lunch, or recess) and go to the nurse's office for "meds." Even in lower grades, the other children will notice this, and there could be some teasing.

"We had (Sean) on Ritalin in kindergarten, and even in kindergarten kids were saying to him, 'Sean, it's time to go take your chill pill,'" recalls Ellen Silva. "I didn't want that when he hit middle school." Sean still takes medication, but he is not on Ritalin, and the drug he takes does not have to be administered during the school day.

(This may be the place to note, as well, that there are forms of Ritalin and Ritalin-like drugs that last longer and do not have to be given to the child during school. In Josh's case, that adjustment did not work well. The alternative drug had some negative effects, and besides, he actually likes taking a break and going to see the nurse every day. So we have kept him on the original dose of Ritalin.)

The medication question is not simply one of Ritalin or nothing, either. Many children on the autism spectrum, including those with AS, take such medications as Dexedrine, Desoxyn (Methamphetamine) or Cylert, in addition to antidepressants, sleep aids and other medications, depending on the child and the situation.

For Maggie Casciato's son Tom, who is now in his twenties, various medications were necessary at certain times of his life, as his development progressed. It was never a simple matter, and was always being reconsidered, she recalls.

"When he was in second or third grade he did take Ritalin, because, like a lot of kids, he benefited from the use of medication to help his attention," Maggie says. "Now, he takes Dexedrine each day. For a while, he was on an antidepressant as well. He was always a quiet kid, kind of withdrawn, but when he reached eleven or twelve, we started to see temper tantrums that were just so unusual. He'd never thrown a temper tantrum before. Here he was, screaming and threatening to hit and banging his hand through walls and things. We went to the same psychiatrist who diagnosed him when Tom was four and said, 'what can we do?' and he put him on (an antidepressant). For many years, he was on an antidepressant. He weaned himself off it; he doesn't like to be on it. He's doing all right without it. But he's been on a few different antidepressants. I found that when he started on Prozac, it changed his ability to socialize; people did notice. He looked them in the eye more often. The way it's supposed to help every-body, it helped him. He still sees the psychiatrist about twice a year."

Anyone who investigates the idea of medication has to be concerned about the possibility of side effects; every drug has some, even if they are extremely minor. Some children who take Ritalin experience "rebound" after the drug leaves their systems, making them more "hyper" and difficult to control than before. There are also reports that some children on Ritalin have trouble falling asleep at night (the drug is, after all, a stimulant) and, in some cases, that a diminished appetite leads to unusually slow or diminished growth.

Josh never experienced a "rebound" from Ritalin, although he did have one when we tried to switch him to Concerta, which has roughly the same effect as Ritalin but lasts longer (thus mak-ing a school time dose unnecessary). Concerta also seemed to depress Josh, making him more moody and sullen than usual during the brief time he was taking it. Within a week, he had returned to the Ritalin dosage he'd been taking before, and the side effects went away.

When he first started taking Ritalin, at age five, Josh some-times had trouble falling asleep at night, but we found that if the medication was not administered later than noon on any given day, that side effect did not seem to surface.

Once again, that is the case with my child, and my child only. Other parents have had different experiences, some posi-tive and some less so.

Ellen Silva's son Sean was taking Concerta until recently, and he did not have the same problems with it that Joshua did.

But when his parents tried him on Ritalin at a younger age, the results were not what they had been hoping for. Sean responded to the medication well enough, but he did have side effects.

"On Ritalin he had a rebound," Ellen recalls. She manipulated his schedule so Sean would not have to take any medication in school, and that meant the rebound could sometimes occur late in the school day, or when Sean was at home. "We had planned (his dosage) for right before he left the house and the minute he walked back the door. (At the time of the interview, Sean was) on an extremely high dose of Concerta; he's on 72 mg. He only weighs 62 lbs. It's almost twice the recommended dose. We have to see the doctors every two months basically because he's on such a high dose. But he is so hyper without the medication; he would be in a special class (without it). There's no way he could be mainstreamed." A few months later, Sean's doctor and his parents decided to try another drug, Adderall XR, at a considerably lower dosage, and Ellen was reporting positive results.

Some parents absolutely reject the idea of medication for Asperger Syndrome. Since they know their children best, it is safe to say that is the right choice for them. In some cases, parents opt to continue with educational and therapeutic options like occupational therapy, speech therapy and social skills training. Others add diet therapies, eliminating such elements as gluten (wheat) and/or dairy products from the child's diet, and they sometimes report very good results with these measures.

There are also parents who combine any or all of these options with medication, and those who opt not to try any therapies but struggling through with behavioral controls and other methods. Medication isn't always the only option, or even the first option. It's one of a number of possibilities; all can be considered, and a specific program for each child should be developed individually, based on the child's personality, needs and tolerances.

The possibility that their children could be on medication for years, and in some cases for life, is a daunting one to many parents. We feel guilty that we are choosing such a course for our children so early in life, and we have a nagging suspicion that if we were really *good* parents, we'd be able to come up with something less intrusive and more effective.

The truth of the matter is that if you have consulted your child's physician, and you trust his or her judgment (if not, you should find a new physician immediately), you can make an educated decision. It's not the first decision you'll have to make for your child, and it won't be the last; it might not even be the most difficult one this year.

When we decided to try a small dosage of Ritalin for Josh in 1996, my wife and I had considerable anxiety about the trial. But we were buoyed by the fact that, as she so aptly pointed out, "If it doesn't help, we can always stop, and it'll be out of his system in three hours." After we determined that Josh was benefiting from the medication, we made sure to check every few months for signs of side effects. And later, we tried other medications on him briefly, but rejected them for the side effects they seemed to cause.

It's going to be your decision, until such time as your child is old and responsible enough to make these choices for him/herself. And it will always be a difficult decision. These days, Josh has been expressing some concern over the pills, and asks frequently why they're necessary. But we see the changes in his mood and behavior on weekends, when he doesn't always get the pills, and so far, we've opted not to stop the medication. Eventually, the drug will probably stop having an effect, and we'll have to make the decision anew. But it shouldn't keep us awake nights, right?

You're Not a Bad Parent If You Cringe

IT WAS A LONG TIME AGO, LONG enough that Josh was actually sitting in the cart as I wheeled it around the local K-mart. He was no older than four, certainly, and perhaps younger. We had collected whatever merchandise we had been dispatched to purchase that evening, and were heading for the cash registers. In the line directly in front of us was a man in his thirties with a muscular build who happened to be African-American.

Four-year-olds have few inhibitions, generally speaking, and Josh, being a four-year-old with Asperger Syndrome (although I didn't know that name at the time), had fewer still. It certainly wasn't the first time he'd seen an African-American man; it wasn't even close. But he seemed fascinated, and stared at the gentleman for some time. Then, he raised his arm and pointed at the man as I hissed that pointing is impolite.

"The man," my son announced in a clear, loud voice, "is brown."

There are moments, raising a child with AS, when you want to drop through a conveniently placed trapdoor and disappear into the night. I remember cringing, and then looking up at the "brown" man in question.

Luckily, he was grinning broadly, and the four or five of us at that cash register had a pretty solid laugh about the incident before buying our merchandise and scattering to the four winds.

Children with Asperger Syndrome sometimes seem impolite, even offensive, when they are simply dealing with the world in the way they see it. In this example, nothing of any consequence happened, nor was there any obvious consequence to Josh's actions. The man in question wasn't offended. But it was, given the context, unusual behavior from a boy Josh's age, and a parent can't always count on the opportunity to explain to those assembled what AS is and why the child might say or do things that aren't socially appropriate.

"Some of the kids with Asperger Syndrome have trouble lying; sometimes they're so literal and they have trouble with theory of mind, the notion that I can understand that you have a different set of beliefs, that I can infer that set of beliefs. I can know that I know something but you don't know it. Somebody has speculated that's why kids with Asperger Syndrome are so literal, because they really can't imagine that what they know is not what's in the other person's head. So they blurt out the truth because they don't know that you can actually deceive someone else," says Dr. Elizabeth Roberts.

The problem isn't that others are judging your parenting skills, but that they don't understand your child's behavior. It's not the judgment you feel; it's frustration at not being able to explain. And all that is compounded by a feeling of guilt that you might not even notice, nor acknowledge, when it surfaces.

You cringed when your child exhibited AS behavior. It's as if you, yourself, didn't understand, and were judging him. So clearly, you are a lousy parent.

It's not unusual to feel that way, even if the feeling isn't entirely rational. In raising *any* child, a parent has to forgive him or herself for not being perfect, just as we do in every other aspect of our lives: we are not perfect in our marriages, in our relationships with family or friends, in our professional undertakings. We're not perfect in the way we eat, the way we talk, the way we dress or even the way we sleep, in all likelihood. Perfection may be the thing we all strive for, but so far, it's been achieved on remarkably few occasions.

In the history of Major League Baseball, there have been fewer than twenty "perfect games" pitched by any player, ever. That means that in the thousands and thousands of games played in the past 140-or-so years, only seventeen times have all the batters on one team been retired by the pitcher without one reaching base. That's a perfect game.

But did any of those pitchers really achieve perfection? Did any of them strike out every single batter he faced without letting any of them hit the ball? Did any of them strike out every batter without ever throwing a pitch out of the strike zone? Of course not. Great fielding plays made by other players helped achieve "perfection," and in some cases umpires might have been called upon to be especially generous with strike calls.

No one, in other words, has ever done anything perfectly. Some people have done things very, very well; some have done them better than anyone else before or since. But never perfectly, not in any field, not in any endeavor. Believe it or not, this is not a perfect book, no matter how much hard work I'm putting into it.

So how, given the fact that parenting is the most difficult job on the planet, and that parenting for a child with AS is *more* difficult by a good margin than it is for a neurotypical child, can we possibly expect ourselves to be perfect as parents? Personally, I'm lucky if I make it through ten straight minutes without screwing something up.

Take a deep breath, because a major truth is coming up in the next phrase: You're *not* a bad parent if you cringe. Read that over a couple of times, because it's true: you are not a bad parent if you cringe.

You are not a bad parent, you're human. It's a natural impulse to feel embarrassment if your child says or does something that is considered inappropriate in the society in which you live. Because children with AS are going to do that on a much more frequent basis than the majority of children, you are going to experience it considerably more often than most parents. If you cringe every once in a while, if you make a face or sigh audibly, you are proving yourself to be a member of the same species as the rest of us. Exhale, smile at your child, and move on.

The concept is the same as forgiving yourself when other parents give you The Look. You don't give society the power over your life to make you feel inadequate as a parent because your child has AS. It doesn't mean that you love your child any less because your first impulse is to react when he does something other people will misinterpret, or something that might illustrate the tendency most children on the autism spectrum have – to see the world as it revolves around them, and exhibit remarkably little empathy for their fellow humans.

It is that trait, the seeming insensitivity to other people's problems, that is most difficult to endure in interactions with those outside the immediate family (and sometimes, with family members who don't understand AS well). Sometimes even we parents have to remind ourselves that our children really *can't* react the same way as we would to a situation, and that they're not simply being self-centered and thoughtless.

A number of years ago, we took a day trip to some historic points in Philadelphia, about ninety minutes from our house. The day had gone well, and we were at our last site, the home of Betsy Ross, when our daughter Eve, who was then five or six, tripped outside the house and cut her head badly on the edge of a marble fountain.

The cut was deep, and Eve was crying. We ran to her, and within minutes an ambulance had been called and we were on our way to the emergency room. In an unfamiliar city, with a little girl who was extremely upset and a pair of parents who weren't far behind, Joshua assessed the situation as we entered the hospital, a bandage absorbing the blood from Eve's forehead.

He looked me in the eye and asked, "How long will we have to be here?"

It was not the best time to ask me that question, but luckily, before I had a chance to hit the ceiling, a friend of ours who was with us offered to take Josh out for ice cream while we saw to Eve's treatment (the wound, by the way, required a few stitches, but Eve was fine, and remains so to this day).

In that case, it wasn't a cringe that was my undesirable reaction; it was something approaching blind fury. Here, my son saw that his sister had been badly hurt, enough to require a trip to the hospital, and his concern was whether we would be back home in time to see his favorite television show that night. I was already upset, and that reaction from my son and his Asperger Syndrome threatened to put me into the stratosphere.

Naturally, later I felt guilty. I hadn't taken Josh's point of view into account; I hadn't been cognizant of his AS at that moment and I had expected from him more than was reasonable to expect. In other words, I'd been just as guilty of not seeing his perspective as he had been of not seeing ours. I think I might have apologized to him later, completely baffling him.

Our feelings as parents come and go in milliseconds; they change twice or three times in the blink of an eye. We are aware of all of them, but we can't hold ourselves accountable for every last emotion that flickers by and dies. Nonetheless, I remember that reaction vividly, and still regret it.

There is no shortcut to forgiving yourself for having the occasional negative thought, but there is a process. First, you have to admit to yourself that such thoughts, such reactions, exist in your mind, even if you reject them immediately. If they don't occur to you ever, and you have a child who has AS, you might not actually be human – and should look into that with your doctor! But if, like the rest of us, you sometimes react with something other than absolute support for your child with AS, you should be aware of a few simple facts:

1. This happens to every last one of us, and the ones who say it doesn't happen to them are lying.
2. Given the huge number of stimuli we encounter in the typical day, your batting average is probably better than .600. Baseball players become obscenely wealthy doing half that well.
3. Your child probably doesn't notice half of the lapses you think you have, and forgets a good half of the others.
4. You can control your emotions, but you can't deny you have them. It's a maintenance problem; you're not a bad person for having feelings.
5. Sometimes, your child really is wrong and your cringe is absolutely justified.

"We've all done things we regretted," says Lori Shery. "We've been wrong many times in what we've done or said. I guess I look at it like I'm human and I'm doing the best I can do. And (Adam is) doing better for me having done what I did than he would if I hadn't done it."

It's not wrong to recognize that you have negative emotions sometimes. It's also not wrong to examine those feelings. To be an effective Asperger parent, we need to be *more* sensitive to feelings, both our own and those of others, than most people are. If some of these emotions lead us to notice our shortcomings, maybe they can help us avoid such problems in the future. But having the feelings themselves can't be counted as a failure; if we noticed our cringes and our mistakes and *didn't* use them to improve our reactions in future scenarios, *that* would be a failure.

Sometimes, the results are subtle, and it's our job to be on the alert and notice them when they occur. Not long ago, my children were going out for the afternoon with their grandmother, a ritual that has been going on weekly for a number of years. It was Eve's turn to choose the activity for the day (this alternating system having been achieved with large amounts of negotiation), and Josh was not pleased with the choice she made. But he knew the rules: s/he who chooses has free reign.

Josh considered being unreasonable about it, and at one point started to melt down in front of my mother, a situation he knows causes me considerable anxiety – that's why he likes to do it. He began to complain about the inequity of the system, stating (incorrectly) that "Evie always gets what she wants, and I have to compromise."

I clenched my teeth, which is a sure sign that I'm going to do something stupid. But having been through this situation before, I took a deep breath, unclenched them after a few moments and said, "Josh, you have a choice. You can go do what Evie wants to do today, and have your own way next time, with no compromises, or you can stay home while she goes and does what she wants."

Josh wanted that to be an unreasonable response, but he couldn't escalate it. After a while, he chose to stay home rather than participate in something that wasn't to his taste. We talked about it later, and things were smoothed over. And I gave myself a very small pat on the back, which is not easy to do when you're sitting down.

We learn from our experiences, or we don't improve.

Debra Schafer is a Pennsylvania-based special education consultant and advocate, and the mother of ten-year-old Evan, who was diagnosed with Asperger Syndrome just before his seventh birthday.

"I've been coaching this parent, and she and I correspond quite frequently via email," Debra explains. "She said, 'I can't take it. I don't understand why (my child) is doing these things, and I just can't seem to get away from it.' I said, 'you know what I want you to do this weekend? I want you to take (your child) out. And I want you to do something like take your child to a toy store, somewhere to just have fun. I want you to just have fun. Forget everything else.' But it's hard, because you do get very wrapped up. Every incremental improvement our kids make is significant beyond anything the parent of a neurologically typical child could see. Whatever our kids would be able to do that seems typical, we make that into the biggest thing. Because it *is* the biggest thing. We have them under a microscope."

Keep in mind that most of the time, it is the anxiety we cause ourselves that does us in. Our children might exhibit what we (and others) consider to be inappropriate behavior, but that doesn't mean we are required to react to it. In the vast majority of cases, the world will most likely continue to rotate on its axis even if our children do flap their hands or say something that seems insensitive to another person.

The notion here is one that runs through the whole of Asperger parenting – *the necessity of choosing one's battles.* If we stop to correct every single one of our children's eccentricities, if we choose to point out every instance in which they act in an unusual or atypical fashion, we are going to spend our lives pointing out inequities and faults. And when we die, all our children will remember of us is that we constantly found fault with them.

Instead, we need to be able to identify the central issues on which we want our children to work. If it's food issues, then concentrate on food issues and let stimming slide for a while. If the behavior you consider most difficult is a lack of empathy, then teach your child the way to at least *appear to* be considering another's point of view. But you can't concentrate on that and worry about his inability to tie his shoes at the same time.

That's not to say that you have to deal with only one issue at a time; it's just that you can't tackle *all* of them at once. It might be best to identify one relatively easy-to-fix issue (say, tying shoes) and work on that at the same time as a more central, "bigger" issue like anxiety over tests in school or aggressive behavior toward other children.

Also, it's important to *prioritize* the issues that you and your child need to address. If this is best for you, write a list on a piece of paper and number the issues. If your child is of school age or older, you might invite him to help compile the list, and ask what his priorities are. You never know for sure what bothers your child, even if you think you do. I'm usually wrong when I guess about such things, and it inevitably comes back to bite me in a place I prefer to remain unbitten.

It's just as crucial to identify those issues you *won't* be addressing now. Make sure you know them backwards and forwards, and that you'll truly be able to ignore the behaviors when you see them. Because once you decide that this will not be on the current agenda, you have to erase it from your mind, and you have to be prepared not to react when it surfaces.

This takes practice, naturally, and the more short-fused among us (and I count myself in that category) have to learn to take a good number of deep breaths, count to whatever number works for us, unclench our teeth and get on with our lives. As a parent, sometimes the things you don't do are more beneficial than the things you do.

All this is easier to recommend than it is to do. But like every other aspect of what we do every day, it takes practice, and with practice, becomes habit. Habits are something with which we should be very familiar. Do what you do with all your other Asperger Syndrome solutions: plan ahead, be ready and stay as patient as you can.

But the most important thing to remember is: *you're not a bad parent if you cringe.*

Time Away From AS

*I*N OCTOBER OF 1994, MY PARENTS and my brother went beyond the limits of generosity and treated my wife and me to an anniversary gift: a four-day trip to Bermuda. We hadn't been away together as a couple since Josh was born five years before, and we had a wonderful time for four days.

But the weeks that led up to that trip were enough to drive us to drink: Josh's preferences were numerous, and even though he and his sister were going to be staying with their grandparents, the preparations necessary to accommodate him were enormous. Foods had to be specified. Things had to happen at exactly the right time of day. Every day. There was a ritual for getting dressed in the morning, one for eating breakfast, one for going to school, one for coming home, and others for eating dinner, taking a bath and (especially) going to bed. All these had to be carefully explained, prepared and shopped for, and then, he had to be reassured that each would be followed to the letter. By the time my wife and I got on that plane, we *needed* a vacation.

We didn't know it yet, but we were about to experience an Asperger Syndrome break. We were taking time off from AS.

Now, a trip to Bermuda is an extreme case (and we have traveled together without our children only once since then, during the writing of this book, for two days), but each parent needs the occasional break. Even parents whose children are neurotypically developing have to find an outlet for themselves, a way to stop being Mom or Dad for a little while and be who they started as in this world. Individually and collectively, parents are also people, and without the means of expressing themselves as individuals, they lose the ability to be the best people they can. In the process, they become less effective parents.

See? You owe it to your child to take a break from him every once in a while. It may seem like a convenient rationalization, but it is true. Give in to an impulse on occasion and become that thinking, vital adult you used to be before you became a Parent (note the capital "P"). It will do everyone some good.

The example above may not be the best one to illustrate this point. An actual vacation from parenting isn't always practical, and it is a bit extreme. On those days when the constant attention to a special interest, the stress of getting through a day of school, the necessary interactions with the school system, the demands on time and thought all seem to be closing in on you, most parents can't just hop the Concorde to Paris and blow off some steam. We usually need to tone down our expectations just a bit.

Besides, a release should be something you can do more regularly, with less planning, and usually for less time than a vacation, even a short one, would entail. Ideally, you'll want something you can do alone *or* with someone else, on short notice, on a regular basis. And it doesn't have to be elaborate; a weekly meeting of a book club can fill the bill nicely.

I have a number of outlets that take me out of the world of AS and into the one I remember from my pre-Josh days. There is work, of course, but that adds its own forms of stress, particularly around deadline times and when waiting for the check to arrive, so it doesn't really count as a form of release.

On the other hand, when I'm not on assignment, I write mystery novels and screenplays "for myself," rather than because they've been ordered. It allows me to let my imagination run wild, to write something I consider enjoyable, and to live, in my mind, in another place, time or situation. For a quick break, there's nothing like fantasy; you can do it anywhere, and nobody even knows you're not really in the same room with them. (As I've said, the hero of my mystery novels does have a son who has AS, and although his personality bears some resemblance to Josh's, he is an exaggerated version of my own son. That's why they call it "fiction," because you make stuff up.)

Those aren't my main avenues of time away from AS, however. Screenplays and novels are too much like work; they involve too much of the same process I use when I'm writing for a living, and sometimes they interfere with the time I spend with Josh after he gets home from school. My real "escapes" are quick, easy to access, and varied: I have a serious need to watch movies on TV; I play acoustic twelve-string guitar, and once a week, I play racquetball.

Each of these three activities fills a specific need in the process of relaxing and removing myself from being an Asperger parent. With movies on tape or DVD, I'm able to take myself to a fantasy world in the same way my own screenplays and novels do, but I don't have to do any of the heavy lifting; someone else has already made up the story and seen to it that it was filmed. The trick for me is to find a time when Josh isn't monopolizing the television to sneak in a movie with my wife, and to avoid being envious of the screenwriter who managed to sell this tedious script while a whole pile of my best work is gathering dust in my filing cabinets. But that's another whole book.

Playing music fills another need. It's easy and instant (I have the guitar right next to my desk, so I can pick it up whenever I want, and while the kids are in school, there is no one in the house to disturb besides the dog, who does not complain too loudly), and it gives me a way to think about something other than work or AS during the average day. Trying to remember a particular chord change or lyric is a welcome relief from IEP meetings, phone calls and emails.

Racquetball is probably the best "mini-vacation" of all, since it requires me to exercise, something I should be doing considerably more often. Once a week, two friends and I get together after dinner and play an hour of racquetball at a gym about thirty minutes from my house. This means I get to see "grownup" friends, exercise, talk about non-parenting-related things, and most important, get out of the house for the better part of an evening. My wife is wonderfully understanding about such things, especially since she does not have a similar weekly activity, although she does run for exercise just about every day.

Other parents I've spoken to make it a point to go out to a movie every week, go bowling, reserve time strictly for reading, skiing, canoeing, singing in a choir, working on home improvements and in one case, flying in a glider once a week. The choice of activity itself doesn't matter; it's the fact of the activity that makes the difference. Just finding a time to do something that *you* want to do because you want to do it can be a liberating idea for a parent whose life seems to revolve around the autism spectrum.

This is not the same issue as tending to your marriage. Yes, it's important to do things together as a couple, and if your time away from AS involves your spouse and you can work out the logistics of it, that's terrific. But if not, if you have something you need to do on your own, if you value your time to "be yourself," then you should be working on your own activity as well as making sure your marriage doesn't suffer from Asperger Syndrome.

There is no telling where an Asperger parent might find a way to have time away. After all, Lori Shery says she found her release valve when she did the one thing that would seem to bring her *closer* to Asperger Syndrome: like Maggie Casciato, Lori started an AS support group, and now ASPEN is the model for such groups around the country. Lori says that starting ASPEN, and now devoting enormous amounts of time and energy to it, really does feed her own need for something that makes Lori feel like Lori.

"I really wanted to be a psychologist," she recalls about her time in high school. "I did candy striping. I worked at (a pediatric psychiatric hospital in New Jersey) when I was in high school. We were told the children were severely emotionally disturbed. They were eight and nine years old. We were also told that they would some day be in an institution, which was so sad. What I've realized since then was that they were autistic. These were children with autism. I remember them looking in the mirror and flapping. They were somewhat verbal, but they were autistic kids. After I worked there for a while, I found it too depressing." Today, Lori is quick to point out, these children would be treated much differently.

Once her son Adam was diagnosed, however, Lori found her true calling, and co-founded ASPEN out of her living room in New Jersey. She now hears from parents from all over the country, most of them dealing with a new diagnosis. Lori's greatest reward is in hearing a parent who was hysterical when Lori answered the phone calm down and have a sense of hope by the time they hang up.

Some people find release in confronting the problems of others, and those of us whom they help are forever grateful.

It sounds so easy: just carve yourself out some time, and take on a hobby. Run. Roller blade. Go to a movie. For people without children, it is easy. Their time is their own, and they can decide how to spend it. For parents of neurotypical children, the demand for free time is heightened, and the ability to spend it lessened. We, the parents of children with AS, have more constraints on our time, increased responsibilities, and less time in which we can loosen up and "be ourselves." Sometimes, paying attention to our children and our relationships with each other can seem to overwhelm any possible time we would spend doing those things we simply like to do.

On an average day, my schedule is roughly as follows: wake at seven, get the kids out of bed. Spend more time with Eve than with Josh, because she has inherited her father's inability to bounce out of bed and get going in the morning. Make lunches for both kids, pack them in backpacks. Help with breakfast when needed (which is most of the time). Get the kids, their homework, backpacks, lunches and assorted accessories out the door by eight. Spend a few minutes checking overnight emails, then walk the dog, who has been patiently waiting on his blanket but isn't in a terrible hurry, since he shares Eve's sleeping pattern in the morning, and doesn't have to go to school.

Next, I drive to the gym, where I spend an hour of time "working on myself," but certainly not enjoying it, since straining muscles and coaxing shortness of breath is not my idea of a good time. Drive home, shower. It is now roughly ten in the morning, and I'm already late for work. That goes on until the kids get home about 2:45. Then, homework, the daily report and then more work until dinner, which is generally my responsibility (along with laundry, but that's not every day).

When my wife gets home, she and I finish making dinner, followed by whatever evening activities (Scout meetings, school meetings, etc.) may be scheduled, then baths or showers for the kids. Then the evening winds down until the kids go to bed around ten, and my wife and I follow about an hour later.

Is there time for me in there? And it should be noted that my schedule is much more flexible than the average commuter, like my wife, who spends at least an hour in the car per day (usually more) and doesn't have the luxury of a kitchen six feet from her office. It's actually much easier for me than it is for most working parents. And my days are still filled before I start thinking about racquetball, guitar or screenplays.

Sometimes, you have to force yourself to take the time. Allow yourself to be a little egocentric, a little selfish. Work something extra into your day, even if it's only for ten minutes. I'm not crazy about working out, and I don't consider it enjoyable, but I do it almost every weekday because I consider it a health issue. Consider your "away time" a mental health issue, and perhaps you can find the time.

It's not always easy. In fact, it's almost never easy.

"I was going to try to walk today," Sharon Graebener said during an interview, when she had been dealing with her son's school district the day before. "Yesterday was so devastating for me. I could try to (handle a school issue), but then there's no time for me. I have no time to exercise or to do something for myself, or to paint some furniture. I feel like I have to take an entire day to prepare for a meeting. I feel like I should really start a diary, but then I would be doing that all day."

It's understandable that most of us feel that way sooner or later. AS adds layers of activity to our days and seems to encroach on unfair amounts of our time. But that only makes it more important for us to take the time, because a stressed-out parent is not as good a parent as one who has the occasional release.

Some Asperger parents, particularly single parents who can't always rely on a partner when the pressure gets too great, find their best refuge behind the nearest closed door. A book and a chair are enough for an escape when twenty minutes is all you can spare and you have to stay in the house. The key is to close the door and make sure you can't be interrupted, even if only for a very brief period.

When you have a couple of hours but can't get out, a rental from the video store can be the tiniest of vacations, but it gets you out of the grind of being an Asperger parent, and recharges your batteries for the next day, the next hour or the next meal, whichever is going to cause the next stress on your nerves.

Going to a parent support group meeting can also be a way to let out all the tension that accrues in our day-to-day existence.

If there is a group in your area, do your best to attend at least one or two meetings. Let out the feelings you thought you had to "hold in" because your co-workers, your friends, even your family members wouldn't entirely understand what it is to have a child with AS. Finding another parent who understands, who has been through what you're going through and may be able to offer advice (or at least empathy) is invaluable.

Ellen Lemma is a single mom, whose son Christopher was eight years old when we talked. She has understanding parents with whom she, Christopher and his brother Alex live, and they often watch the children for an evening so Ellen can get out and let off a little steam.

"I have an excellent group of friends," Ellen says. "I have one friend I've been friends with since high school and she's always there for me. I have another group of friends I met about a year ago. We met through special ed workshops that I've gone to, and we get together on average once a month; we call it the Happiness Club. Each of our children has some kind of disability, and it's almost like a mini-support group. Whoever needs help that month gets it, and if nobody needs it, we sit around and laugh. Whether we're laughing or crying, it's a great outlet because the people in that group truly understand what you're going through."

Many "mini-vacations" require the services of a babysitter – a term I come to hate more with each passing year. My children are not babies, but I would not leave them alone in the house for more than a very short time, and until Josh turned twelve this year, it was illegal for me to do so. Finding a sitter is not always the easiest thing to organize. A good sitter also costs more money than an inexperienced one. But finding someone who can stay with a child who has AS and understand the situation is, to paraphrase the credit card ad, "priceless."

Usually, the best alternative is to have a family member or friend, someone your child knows well, and who knows your child well, stay with your child while you're out. This is the most workable alternative for many families because it requires the least amount of prior preparation for both the sitter and the child. It also allows the child to adhere to his usual routine, which can be a huge issue for our kids. And it is usually free, which can be a pretty serious issue for adults.

A sitter who is not a close friend or family member has to be well prepared ahead of time for the rituals and demands a child with AS might present, and should be educated as to what those funny words "Asperger Syndrome" mean. It's not necessary to haul out textbooks and quiz someone who is going to be watching your child for a few hours, but the basics, as they apply to the amount of time in question, should be addressed.

It can be helpful to look at a nearby college or university for students, particularly in the education or psychology departments, who might have some background in special education or autism spectrum disorders. Some states have programs that match up qualified sitters with parents who need someone to watch a child with a disability, but they usually are designed for times when the parent needs to work, rather than indulge in some "away time." Check with your state's department of social services for information.

Also, consult with other Asperger parents for recommendations; there is usually a grapevine of parents who know the best sitters in the area. They might cost a bit more, but the odds are the time you spend tending to yourself will be worth it.

Get out there and _____ (fill in the blank)!

Single Parents Have It Twice As Hard

*Y*OU'VE EXPERIENCED THE DIFFI-
culties, both physical and emotional, that Asperger Syndrome
can bring to a parent. You know that each day can be a trial, a
triumph, a marathon or a sprint, and you know that it's not going
to get any easier any time soon. You have worried yourself to
sleep, gotten up in the middle of the night and pulled yourself
through a day during which your child will challenge you, intentionally or not, at every turn. You have been exhausted, exhila-
rated, debilitated, frightened – and just plain worn out. And you
have managed, through it all, to maintain your composure most
of the time and to feel that, as each day goes by, maybe you're
becoming a better parent. But boy, are some of those days tough.

Now, imagine you're doing it alone.

The one thing that parents who live together can almost
always count on is that there will be backup. If one parent can't

answer the bell for a particular crisis, the other will be there to fill in, usually without having to discuss it first. There is always one other person who knows all the things you know, who doesn't need any explanation and can do, essentially, what you would do in any given situation. The other parent will be there to bail you out when the stress is too much, or when your particular parenting gifts aren't appropriate to the situation. In other words, there is always someone there to pick up the slack for you.

Single parents have it twice as hard. And that's probably an underestimate.

"It's harder to be a single parent, period, with any child. And then if the child has significant disruptive behaviors it's that much more difficult," says Dr. Jed Baker. "The children of single parents that I've known tend to be more withdrawn, and I don't think it was significantly more difficult in certain ways because the kids tended to be the ones who did not have meltdowns and temper tantrums, but were more shy and withdrawn. If you have a youngster who does have a lot of impulse control problems and is prone to meltdowns, if you have a combination of being both frustrated easily and having some skill difficulties that are going to make you more likely to run against an obstacle and be frustrated, then you're going to be prone to meltdowns. That's got to be harder if you're a single parent."

Most Asperger parents are like trapeze artists working without a net. Single Asperger parents are like trapeze artists working without the other person to catch you when you swing out. It's a significant difference, I think you'll agree.

While there is little statistical data on the subject, anecdotal evidence suggests that there is a relatively high divorce rate among Asperger parents. This, coupled with the fact that the divorce rate for the overall population is already high (The National Center for Health Statistics reported 957,200 divorces, excluding California, Indiana and Louisiana, in the United States in 2000), means there are a good number of single Asperger parents around. Consider also that some Asperger parents never married, and the number increases.

Physically, emotionally and financially, single parents face more difficulties than those who can rely on another adult. Add in the factor of a child with Asperger Syndrome, and the difficulty level increases substantially. Those who are going at it on their own are doing so with the bar raised higher, and no one to act as spotter.

"Single parents really are carrying the entire burden – emotional, physical, sometimes financial. And they just don't get a break," says Lori Shery. "Fortunately, a number of them have a family member in the area who does help out, but it's not the same as having somebody living with you full-time who shares responsibility. I give them a lot of credit, because I think they're really strong, and they have to be. It's overwhelming for them. They can come to the support group meetings, try to meet up with other single parents, usually single parents of children with issues, but they need to take care of themselves as an individual. They're not just a mommy or a daddy. Whether it's taking time at night to talk to someone or read a book, or on the weekends just going to the mall or do something relaxing, it's important. I know some of the parents have connected up, and I think some of them have even arranged for one family to watch the kids for a couple of hours and then the others watch for a couple of hours to give them a break."

The difference comes in having to deal with *everything*: all the school meetings, all the temper tantrums, all the decisions, all the financial responsibilities; they all fall on the single parent. Each time there's a question, the single parent has to answer; there can be no deferring to the other parent. Every time the child with AS is in a cranky mood, the single parent will bear the brunt of the attack. Every meal is prepared, every outing planned, every vacation explained to the child with AS by one parent, not two.

Granted, a good many divorces end with some form of joint custody these days, and ex-spouses don't always disappear from the life of their children. But during the times when one or the other parent is living with the child with AS, he or she is the sole person responsible. There is no "tag-team" effect, where one parent who has had enough for one day can pass responsibility for the rest of the night to a partner. If you've had a bad day at work, you still have to deal with your child's Asperger Syndrome. You can't ask your spouse to do it for you, just for a little while.

Many divorced, widowed and simply single Asperger parents live with or near a family member – a parent, a sibling or someone else close to the Asperger parent – and share some of the responsibility for raising the child. Day care can be expensive, and a helpful grandparent at home after school can be invaluable.

"(My sons) have their grandparents, whom they adore, and I get my support system, too. It's a constant struggle, but we get through it," says Ellen Lemma, whose divorce proceedings began a week after her son Christopher, then not yet six, was diagnosed. "I do a lot that is related to Asperger Syndrome, and every now and then I need to turn it off because it becomes overwhelming, and my mother has been very good about that." Ellen lives with her parents in New York City.

But there are those who don't have a backup system, and who can't afford to pay for full-time day care or after-school care. Financial worries, which can often be tied to a divorce or death in the family, are exacerbated in a family with a child who has special needs. Nothing comes for free, outside the public school system. And even that isn't always as accommodating as it could be.

There are programs at the municipal, state and federal levels that offer some help, but autism spectrum disorders are not usually at the top of the list for aid. Financial aid can come from family, as well, but there are no easy answers. And money is not always the core of the problem, either. In many cases, the parent's emotional state is more brittle when he or she has to deal with every situation alone. Financial troubles are a very heavy burden, but they are not the only burden.

Single parents, because they bear more of the responsibility individually than either parent in a two-parent household, are more susceptible to the pressures and stresses of being an Asperger parent. Everything requires more effort; everything seems to be more difficult, even when it's not. But there are many single Asperger parents who cope remarkably well, some getting involved in the effort to help all Asperger parents with the day-to-day situations that evolve.

"Sometimes," says one single mother I've met, "dealing with other people's problems makes me feel like mine aren't so bad. It's awful to say, but there's some comfort in seeing people who are actually worse off than you are."

Ellen Lemma takes the occasional night out with friends to "decompress," and finds that to be the kind of "vacation from AS" that all Asperger parents – perhaps the single ones most of all – need.

"I get together with some of my friends, and I have a chance to be myself for an evening," Ellen reports. "It makes a really big difference."

I have no experience as a single parent, other than those rare occasions when my wife is traveling for business, and that doesn't really count, since I know she'll be home in, at most, a few days. But that taste of the added responsibility and the absence of a break is enough for me to know that I don't envy the life of the single Asperger parent.

Granted, my financial burden is the same when my wife is home and when she's traveling, but the rest of the single parent life is at least viewable during times when one parent isn't able to be home. Instead of being able to rely on someone else to help with dinner, to herd the children toward their beds at the proper time, and to defuse a situation when one is brewing, I have to rely strictly on myself. And I'm not all that reliable.

The practical difference isn't all that great, since the situation rarely lasts for more than a day or two. But the emotional stress is palpable, even if it doesn't manifest itself at any given moment. It's the fact that I know there isn't anyone to turn to that registers emotionally; and even when the kids are on their best behavior (they do tend to rise to the occasion), there's always the nagging feeling in the back of my mind that any time one of them calls for a parent, I'm the one answering the call. No exceptions.

When I multiply that situation from a day or two to every day, all the time, I get a taste of what the single Asperger parent has to deal with. And I marvel at the ones I know who do it so well.

Dating and the Single Asperger Parent

I am especially in awe of the single Asperger parent when I consider that, in addition to all the things I have to do when I'm on my own with the children, the single parent in question has made the decision to try dating again.

Dating for a single person in general is a difficult proposition. Add a divorce or widowhood to that proposition, and the difficulty increases by a wide margin. It increases again when a child or more is involved, and when at least one child has Asperger Syndrome, the difficulty increases geometrically once again.

Think about how hard it is for you to explain AS to friends who haven't encountered it before. Think about how tough it is/was for you to go on *any* first date. And now add the two things together, and you'll begin to see the obstacles that single Asperger parents face. It's not an idyllic picture, by any means.

One single mother I know told me she hasn't considered dating for exactly that reason. "I can't even think about it," she says. "It's hard enough just trying to get through the average day, without having to think about getting someone to watch my son, and then thinking about all the things you need to think about on a first date, and *then* having to tell whoever this person is about Asperger Syndrome. I'm not ashamed of (my son), but by the end of the day, I'm too tired to have to explain this whole complicated condition to a stranger and be charming at the same time."

Ellen Lemma, whose marriage broke up almost at the same time her son Christopher was diagnosed in 1999, says she's barely stuck a toe in the dating pool since then. "I've literally gone out on one date. He was a nice guy, but it was blind date, and he was not my cup of tea. I would date, and my parents are very supportive of that whole thing. I definitely can, but I just don't have the same opportunities. I'm a teacher of autistic preschoolers in their homes. So guess how many opportunities I have to meet single, available men at work? If it happens, it happens, and if it doesn't, it doesn't. I'm not going to let it take over my life. It's not something I would share with my kids."

While she does want to start dating again, Ellen has reservations about the process. Since her marriage ended, she says her focus has been on her two sons. "We broke up in November of 1999, so it's been two and a half years now. I know the reason I'm not out there is, as my girlfriends tell me, 'you don't put yourself out in situations where you can meet people.' Well, does that mean going out to bars and just hanging out? I didn't like that when I was twenty-one! I just don't have the patience anymore. My patience is used for other things. If the opportunity comes my way, I'd start dating again."

Any single parent has to prepare a child for the prospect of the parent dating again. With a child who has Asperger Syndrome, the preparation, like preparation for anything else, must be considerably more detailed and much more intense.

"There are two ways to think about this: kids on the spectrum are just like any other kids, which is to say that just because they have a diagnosis of an autism spectrum disorder doesn't mean they're also not going to be prone to the jealousy and the upsets that surround parents starting to date again," Dr. Baker says. "On the other hand, there are some kids, because of their autism spectrum disorder, who seem less concerned about some of these issues than their typical peers would have been. They're much more concerned about whether or not they'll be able to continue to watch *Pokémon*. They're not really concerned about the sort of notion that mom's dating this guy and that's somehow a betrayal of my father. That's an abstract concept, and there are some kids who are immediately going to grasp that, and so they're upset: 'If I like this guy, that's like betraying my father.'"

The situation can become more difficult between the Asperger parent and the new adult in the child's life when the new boyfriend or girlfriend doesn't understand the disorder, and becomes one of the people who might otherwise have wielded The Look.

"A lot of the stepparents don't immediately get the idea that this is a special needs youngster," Jed Baker explains. "As a result, they may think maybe you're just spoiling the child and maybe they want to come in and be the disciplinarian, and that requires some adult discussion. Sometimes they're right, but there needs to be some discussion about the time when we need to accommodate to this child because she really does have a disability versus the time we want to impose consequences. It amplifies some normal stepparenting issues when you have a child with a disability."

In short, dating situations are, like many situations with autism spectrum disorders, the same as they would be for parents of neurotypical children – except *more*. Any child whose parents split up needs to have the situation explained, but a child with AS needs it explained in a more specific context. Any child of divorce or widowhood will have issues when his or her parent starts seeing someone new – but a child with AS might complicate the situation by failing to acknowledge them or by needing more attention at a time when his primary caretaker is trying to divide time between the existing family and a new relationship. Nothing is simple.

A responsible Asperger parent will know that introducing a new adult into a child's life should never been done until it's a reasonably sure bet that adult will be involved with the child and his family for a long period of time. The explanation of AS to the new prospective relationship should begin relatively soon, since the adult who has not been an Asperger parent before will probably require some introduction to the disorder and explanations of the specific accommodations that need to be made for the child. The new boy/girlfriend's reaction to those accommodations and the disorder itself can be difficult, and such reactions have been known to torpedo budding relationships when the "new" adult is not able to understand.

"There are lots of issues in these situations. Is the new boyfriend or girlfriend taking on a disciplinary role? Is it too early to do that?" asks Dr. Baker. "Have they built up any credit with this youngster first? Is the new boyfriend or girlfriend taking a lot of time away from special time between mom and the child or dad and the child? This is especially true when they've already spent some time where it was just mom and the kids, and now a new boyfriend comes in and mom is spending more time with the boyfriend."

Solutions, or at least ways to deal with such problems, are the same as they would be with a neurotypical child, but as always, more complex for a child with AS. "There are concrete things you can do, like making sure there's special time for the custodial parent and the child aside from time with the boyfriend," says Dr. Baker. "For that matter, take some time to build a relationship with the stepparent or whomever. I think it's wise not to introduce that until you're sure it's going to be a steady thing."

The issues with new adults entering the child's life can be difficult, but like anything else the single Asperger parent encounters, they become less so with practice. The first date after not going out for years might be a rough one, but maybe the fourth or fifth won't be as difficult. Maybe it's hard to get all the money together for the bills this month, but it always seems to come out even in the end. These problems are far from trivial – they can be devastating – but they are the same problems, only magnified by the emphasis on one person's responsibility.

The trick, as with all other Asperger parenting issues, is to keep a clear head, which is far easier written than done. Juggling all the responsibilities of being an Asperger parent, along with the needs and emotional changes that accompany a single parenting situation of any kind, takes an enormous amount of discipline and control, which can be hard to come by at the end of a long day. I'm not able to speak from experience; I can only report what the single Asperger parents I know tell me, and that is: it seems to be there when you need it most. That's not scientific, it's not even logical, but it appears to be true.

Single parents have it twice as hard, and yet they seem to navigate the choppier waters with grace and serenity most of the time. It is impossible not to admire that.

You Got a Problem With It?

*T*HERE ARE TWO KINDS OF PARENTS (non-Asperger parents) who tend to give us The Look. The first is the kind of adult who sees us enduring a meltdown at the shopping mall or in a restaurant, or worse yet, a friend who sees it going on during a visit to our home, and feels compelled to explain to us how to discipline our children.

It's not easy, but you really do have to curb your impulse to strangle them.

A friend of mine, the publicist and author Michael Levine in Los Angeles, has a view of life he calls The Ambassador Theory. Michael says (and he wrote about this in his book *Raise Your Social I.Q.*) that each of us, when we leave our homes every day, acts as an ambassador for a number of different groups, whether we like it or not. For example, by Michael's definition, I would be an ambassador for the male gender, for Jewish people, for New

Jerseyans, for parents, for fathers and for people under average height. As such, I must keep in mind when I deal with people during the average day that they see me in any one or more of those roles, and probably ones I haven't thought of. If I do something that offends them, for example, they might think, "all New Jerseyans are so *rude*." When the truth is, only most of us are.

Acting as an ambassador, then, helps us to react to some of the situations we encounter as we go about our lives. If we think like ambassadors in all relationships, we'll have an easier time maintaining our control than if we were thinking like normal civilians. Try not to notice that other people aren't acting like ambassadors so much when they deal with you; it'll only make your head hurt.

We are, each of us, ambassadors for the country of Asperger Syndrome. Like it or not, we are the ones who will be consulted whenever the subject of AS is brought up in other people's homes, when a question is raised, when somebody's nephew's friend's insurance agent's mother believes her grandchild might have Asperger Syndrome. Once we identify ourselves as Asperger parents, we are in essence proclaiming our allegiance to that country and announcing our appointment to the ambassadorship.

In other words, expect to hear about AS a lot from people who, on a basic, fundamental level, don't understand it at all.

They will offer theories; they will refer to half-remembered magazine articles. Parents of neurotypical children will give advice on child rearing and propose that your child is "going through a phase." They will remark that you should do one thing or another, or merely imply such suggestions by announcing, while your child is having a full-fledged meltdown over the wrong kind of Parmesan cheese on his pasta, that their children used to act like this until they, the parents, learned how to get tough in a constructive way.

Again, keep in mind that actual physical violence is illegal, and in most cases doesn't make the victim any smarter or more compassionate than he was before. And, we are not the kind of ambassadors who benefit from diplomatic immunity. No, there has to be another way. And there is.

Education, education, education.

Even on the days when you feel like you've explained Asperger Syndrome to every person on the face of the planet, rest assured there are still millions out there who haven't heard those two words yet, and don't have the slightest idea why your son won't wear corduroy pants because they make an annoying sound. These are the people with whom your child will have to study, work, play and live with for the rest of his life, so the sooner they start getting the message, the better his life is going to be. It's going to take a long time to educate every person on earth, so let's get started.

First of all, we have to eliminate the jargon that we as a sub-culture have developed. Sure, *you* know what a "neurotypical" child is, but the parents of neurotypical children probably don't. You might be able to tell someone that AS is an autism spectrum disorder that generally falls into the mid-functioning or high-functioning areas of the continuum, but if you say that too many times to people who aren't in the autism community, you're likely to run into a good many glassy stares, and you won't have educated a whole lot of people.

Instead, say that your child has a condition called Asperger Syndrome, which is like autism, except that "autism" is a very wide-ranging type of condition, and not one specific thing. Explain that your child (in all likelihood) does speak, but that he doesn't process information the same way most of us do, and might not understand body language or idioms like "you're pulling my leg" because he takes most expressions literally. Then explain each of your child's external "symptoms," whatever they may be, in terms that people who have not dealt with this disorder before will find familiar.

Second, we cannot rely on the news media to do our job for us. As a freelance reporter, it pains me to say so, but the media generally doesn't get the story right when dealing with autism spectrum disorders in general, and AS in particular. And because of the realities of the news business, where a more "dramatic" story is better than a more accurate one, and (in TV especially) where a strong visual makes a better story than detailed information, the story will often be either overdramatized (the "smiling-through-the-tears" story) or oversimplified to the point that no real information is communicated.

The problem with that is that most viewers, readers or listeners will remember only the most striking nuggets of information presented, and the vast majority of them will not be interested enough to do follow-up research on the Internet, in books or elsewhere.

A couple of years ago, a nationally broadcast news magazine show was preparing a report on AS, and contacted Lori Shery, who suggested they get in touch with my wife and me to see if Josh might be included in the piece they were discussing. The producer of the segment called and asked for a "snapshot" of what Josh was like.

I explained that Josh is a high-functioning child with Asperger Syndrome, that he is included in a "mainstream" class with an aide, and that – and this is what doomed his participation in the television segment entirely – an adult who met with him for a short period of time "probably wouldn't notice a dramatic difference in him."

You could hear the enthusiasm wane over the phone, which was fine, since I wasn't one hundred percent sure I wanted my son's face broadcast on a major television network in prime time. But the producer, who wanted something more striking and "dramatic," not to mention visual, for her segment, was clearly disappointed that Josh wouldn't be doing anything "unusual" if the crew showed up at our house. We parted company amicably. The segment aired later that year, and was, to be honest, quite good for what it communicated. It was, given the realities of network television, a bit compressed and simplistic, but it probably couldn't avoid that. The children profiled had noticeable tics and stimmed quite a bit, and each had a very specific special interest, something Josh has never really developed.

The point is that the news media will occasionally pay attention to autism spectrum disorders, particularly as the number of diagnoses continues to grow each year. But we can't depend upon the media to deliver our message for us, and we can't control the message the media will send. In our personal lives, we have to present our own information in our own way, to the people around us who mean something in our lives.

Third, we can't expect everyone we know, even our close family, to become experts on AS on the spot. This is not an "obvious" disorder, although it is far from the "invisible" condition we hear about. Still, it takes a little subtlety to understand it, and the finer points will not be evident even on first explanation. There will be a learning period for anyone involved. Think how long it took before *you* understood what Asperger Syndrome is, <u>really</u>.

You can't expect to change the world in an afternoon; it took at least a week to make it, after all. And we don't have the same resources as the crew that performed that task.

In the six years from 1996 to 2001, the New York Yankees appeared in the World Series five times and won four, a remarkable record. And it coincided with the stewardship of manager Joe Torre, who said he told his players not to worry about hitting a home run every time they came to bat. "Think in small bites," Torre said he told the Yankees, and it worked consistently in a sport that demands consistency above all else.

We need to think in small bites, too. We have to talk to our family, our friends, our neighbors and our acquaintances one at a time or in very small groups. We have to know what we're going to say and how we're going to explain it. We need to achieve an emotional "even keel" that will deflect any inconsiderate or insensitive comments or actions by the people who are being introduced to Asperger Syndrome for the first time. None of this is easy, but luckily, it draws on the one skill that any

Asperger parent should have developed to the level of high art: the ability to *prepare*.

The first step, you'll recall, is understanding the condition yourself, and understanding that your child is not alone with it. Neither are you. Support group meetings reinforce that, and can give you strong ideas on how to introduce and explain AS to people who have not been exposed to it before.

"One of the benefits of attending a support group is finding out you're not alone," says Lori Shery. "You're sitting there saying, 'my kid did this.' And you're hearing, 'yeah, my kid does that too. Wait'll you see what my kid did.' And you're starting to realize, OK, my child is different, and he has problems and if people are going to judge him and be nasty about it, then they are the ones with the problem."

Of course, there are all sorts of ways to react to such stimuli. If someone doesn't understand AS and attempts to lecture you on your child-rearing skills, you can choose to stamp your foot and scream, you can deliver your own lecture on autism spectrum disorders and their pervasive nature in society, or you can try to explain in calm, measured tones the possibility that the person has misconstrued the situation.

In the past few years, Asperger Syndrome has gained a good deal of news coverage in print and broadcast media, and public awareness, although still far from strong, has increased somewhat. Everyone seems to know *somebody* who is in some way connected to AS: a relative, a friend or some co-worker is probably related to someone who has Asperger Syndrome. So the incidents of uninformed people misjudging a situation in public are not as common as they used to be.

Still, the situation is far from resolved, and Asperger Syndrome is not at all a household term. So, in our role as ambassadors of AS, we need to keep our own behavior in mind when we react to a person who might not understand exactly what we're dealing with during a public "scene" or a total meltdown.

"I know some organizations – and I personally don't believe in this – that actually have little cards made up that say on the outside: 'if my child's behavior is surprising to you,' and you open it up and it says, 'it's because he's autistic. Don't judge him.' That to me is confrontational," Lori Shery says.

Indeed, if we all walk around with a chip on our shoulders waiting for the neurotypical community to knock it off, we're not good ambassadors and we're not going to progress in achieving our goal. Education isn't best accomplished with a whip and a chair, unless your students happen to be Bengal tigers.

Sometimes, I find it's easier if we deal with those who would challenge our ability to deal with our children as if *they* were the people with Asperger Syndrome. Use the skills you've developed in talking to your child when you discuss his disorder with other adults, and you'll find yourself staying calm, explaining in clear, concise terminology and many times being more effective than if you let your emotions reign.

Now, I'm not suggesting for a moment that such a thing is easy. I'm an expert at letting my emotions get the best of me, but when the moment arrives, I find that the ability to stop, take a breath, and *then* react is invaluable. It isn't the way I always manage to do, but it is what I'm always striving to do.

Remember, people who challenge us – directly or indirectly, since direct confrontations are rare – are not really trying to tell us that we're bad parents. In most cases, The Look doesn't mean what we think it means. Strangers are not, as a rule, interested enough in our lives to interfere with them. We have to be able to distinguish between the times when someone is really confronting us and questioning our ability to raise our children (at least in that moment) and the times when we simply feel exposed, the times when we're embarrassed because our children will not hesitate to "make a scene" in public. Because ninety percent of the time, the rest of the world is far too busy obsessing about its own life to notice, let alone interfere with, ours.

Keep in mind what Dr. Baker said earlier: *we* decide how much power we're going to give to other people. If we determine that they don't understand, and we can help educate them, we are trying to help the entire autism spectrum community. But if we happen to be less confrontational types who prefer to avoid such moments, it is just as constructive to simply refuse to endow others with enough authority to make us feel bad about our parenting skills. So long as we know we're doing the right thing in the situation, there is no reason to worry about what others, especially strangers, think.

Friends and (especially) relatives are a different story, since they have a much more significant impact on our emotional lives than people we've never met before. When we are met with disapproval from those close to us, we tend to react more deeply. But first, we have to determine whether that disapproval is real, or whether we're simply projecting the reaction we *think* we will get before it actually occurs.

If your four-year-old is squirming and cranky while you're trying to tie his shoes, moving his feet and complaining, and your emotional temperature is rising, you might be likely to raise the volume of your pleas to "sit still" just a bit. If your mother, visiting for the day, walks over at that point and says, "hold on," you could quite logically assume she's disapproving of your tactics and react sharply at her.

But if you take a moment at that point, you might see that your mother is simply walking over to help tie the shoe you're not working on at the moment and speed up the process. It's important not to react to a situation that is not what it appears to be, and not to give in to the natural impulse, which is to believe that no one but you understands your child's AS, so therefore no one but you can provide the proper solution to any given situation.

Sometimes, a relative or friend really doesn't understand, and really is challenging the way you are reacting to a given moment. But it is only about that moment, not about your overall skill as a parent. No matter what history there is between you, don't try to connect everything to a larger picture. If there are issues that need to be dealt with, perhaps a professional therapist should be consulted. But if it's just about this moment, this day, right now, accept the suggestion for what it is. You don't have to agree with it, but you can understand it.

That cleansing breath, the thing they taught you about in Lamaze class when you were getting ready to have your child, is the key. Take a good deep breath before reacting to any situation and you'll have a more measured, considered response. That works for situations with your child, and with the people who might (or might not) be challenging your tactics in raising him.

The hard part, of course, is remembering to take the breath. It takes practice. And remember that those close to you probably aren't trying to criticize as much as you think they are; they're interested in your family, and they don't understand AS the way you do. Education is important for the "outside" world, but it is that much more important for those who are closest to you and your child with Asperger Syndrome.

This gets back to the issue of "coming out" with AS. For those who choose not to make the child's condition "public" with friends and family, more situations that seem confrontational will probably arise. It becomes a matter of importance to explain why you react to your child's behavior the way you do (and for that matter why the child behaves that way to begin with) in order to be understood. It can lower the emotional temperature in exchanges between you and those whom you believe are judging you, and it can just as easily reduce the number of such exchanges.

Everybody's not watching you. It just feels that way. But with honesty, education and that ultra-important moment when you take a breath, you might be able to think just a little more clearly. And wouldn't *that* be nice?

So How Is Josh?

*T*HERE IS SOMEONE WHO LIVES IN MY town (whom I will not name) who has known Josh and our family since we moved here, when Josh was four years old. We met right around the time Josh was diagnosed, and we were learning about Asperger Syndrome and what it meant to his life. At the time, Josh was trying to make friends with this woman's son, who is roughly his age, and without the social skills training he would eventually receive, he wasn't doing a very good job of it. There is no animosity involved, but the two boys never became friends.

Since the time Joshua began kindergarten, there hasn't been an instance when I met this woman on the street and she didn't begin by grasping my hand in both of hers, giving me her best sad-eyed, sympathetic look, and asking in a heart-rending voice, "So how *is* Josh?"

To this point, I have refrained from physical violence, but I make no guarantees for the future. So far, I have had the presence of mind to answer, "He's fine. How is (her son)?"

She looks startled that I would ask. "Oh, he's doing fine," she'll say. "But how is Josh *doing?*"

"Fine. How are *you* doing?"

It goes on from there. And rarely does the conversation progress.

The flip side of The Look is The Mope, that supposedly sympathetic stare you get from parents who know your child has Asperger Syndrome and think that this means you are any number of famous martyrs rolled into one. They compliment your "strength," ask how you are "battling this disease," and in a variety of other ways intimate that you should be commended for the heroic way in which you are facing this test of your mettle.

Give me a break.

Asperger Syndrome is a disorder that, depending on the degree to which your child is affected, can create challenges for your child to overcome. These can range from a few adjustments in the classroom to more serious accommodations that will be needed for a lifetime, including (in some cases) living assistance, difficulties with peers and finding a mate, possible entanglements with uninformed members of law enforcement agencies and bouts with depression and uncertainty. That's a worst-case scenario.

It is *not* a life-threatening illness. It is not a "disease" that other people can catch. It does not require physical adjustments, crutches, wheelchairs, surgery or, in many cases, even medication. We parents may face some different challenges than others, but in most cases what we face are the usual challenges, amplified. If neurotypical children become rebellious at puberty, we can expect our kids to become downright belligerent. When they are toddlers, our children need to be taught about body language, idioms and facial expressions. They have to be shown how to make eye contact. They require specific and unusual methods of teaching in the classroom, and sometimes they need accommodations. Maybe they won't eat the same number of foods as neurotypical kids, or they'll be more adamant about the way their meals are prepared. This makes their lives – and ours – more challenging, certainly.

But we are not the objects of pity. We don't need sympathy, although empathy wouldn't be an awful thing. We don't require the basset-hound look in another parent's eyes that says, "You poor thing, how you suffer with that afflicted child of yours." Please. Save your sympathy for someone who needs it and help me convince a balky school system (not my own, which is very accommodating, I hasten to add) to include more special needs kids.

Can you tell we've reached a bit of a sore point for me?

The Mope is an attempt by a neurotypical parent (or nonparent) to relate to an Asperger parent. It is a way of reaching out, but it is done in a way that communicates a sense of superiority, focusing on us "unlucky" sorts to whom the Fates have been unkind. It is exactly the kind of thing Asperger parents don't need, since it leads to our wallowing in self-pity rather than focusing on what needs to be done. And worst of all, it is aimed at the wrong group. We have a heavy workload, sure, but we aren't in such awful shape that we need to be pitied.

One Asperger mother I know positively bristles when a member of her family compliments her on "the fine job you're doing raising (her son)." "I know (the family member) means it to be a compliment," the Asperger mom says, "but I also hear the way (the family member) emphasizes the *fine job*, and I know it wouldn't be said that way if (my son) were neurotypical. I have to bite my tongue to stop from telling her not to say that."

If we are open and honest with our family and friends, they should know there is no reason to feel sorry for us. But if we've been hiding our children's AS, if we have been treating the disorder as something to feel ashamed of, it is understandable that those close to us might treat it that way.

We each deal with The Mope differently, depending on our natural temperament, the type of day we're having, our relationship with the person who is Moping, and how many times we've seen The Mope this week. Confronted with stares in public places, we are going to go off like a rocket, try to explain and overcompensate, or deal with it in a manner that is unique to ourselves.

"Most of the time, I just explain to them that my son is autistic," says Ellen Silva. "Then they say he's doing so well, and I say, 'yes he is doing well,' because they don't know what Asperger Syndrome is. If someone becomes a close friend, I'll explain more to them, but if I tell them he's autistic, they think he's doing great for an child with autism."

Self-esteem is a tricky issue with any person. An Asperger parent, when first confronted with the disorder, has a number of changes to undergo, not the least of which is an examination of self-image, and self-esteem plays a huge part in that examination. If we believe that there is something "wrong" with our children, and that, given the evidence that there is a genetic link, it is somehow "our fault," we are likely to feel inadequate, and therefore may try to hide or conceal our children's AS. However, most Asperger parents, after a reasonable period of time, realize that AS is not something to be ashamed of, that it isn't anybody's "fault," and that there is no reason to hide it. Once we reach that level of self-awareness, we can usually deal with the uninformed relatively well.

"Coming out" about AS is usually the first step. Some Asperger parents actually hold a family meeting and explain the condition, making it clear that this is not something to mourn and that the child's life is not ruined. If relatives and close friends understand what they're being told, and go through the same period of adjustment the parents did, it is usually the case that they accept the fact of the disorder and move on.

Debra Schafer, Asperger parent and special education advocate, says she understands why some Asperger parents are testy with those who express sympathy, rather than empathy. "I think parents chafe for a number of reasons. No one likes to feel pitied," she says. "No one likes to feel as if people are feeling sorry for them. That's a dreadful way to feel. A lot of people do feel sad for us. And there's nothing to feel sad about."

It is that realization – that there actually is nothing to feel sad about – that is most difficult for new Asperger parents, and then their relatives, friends and acquaintances. Once that realization is achieved, however, it is much easier to deal with people who have no background in AS and don't understand enough about it to react the way we react.

Remember, to most people, the word "autism" is extremely dramatic and upsetting. Think about the first time you heard it associated with your child. The images we've been given of people with autism and the experiences we have had with those we might have known have colored our view of the spectrum. In all likelihood, the first time we were confronted with the word "autism," we weren't aware there was such a thing as a "spectrum." We thought everyone who was autistic was like Dustin Hoffman in *Rain Man*.

When Lori Shery's son Adam first exhibited signs of difficulty, she and her husband Steven had Adam examined by a neurologist, and when Lori read the doctor's report, it hit her very, very hard. "In the report it said, 'Adam should be monitored for the possibility of a pervasive developmental disorder,'" she recalls. "I didn't know what that was so I looked it up in Steven's medical book and freaked out. Hysterical, I called the neurologist and said, 'What do you mean he may be autistic?' Because this is what I knew of autism: when I was a teenager, my parents' friends who lived in another town had a son who was probably four years older than me, and he was autistic. He used to spend the day in the swimming pool and walk around the periphery splashing the water and going 'ahhhhh.' That's what autism was to me."

Keep in mind, Lori went on to overcome her panic, learn about autism spectrum disorders, co-found ASPEN and raise her son, now a teenager, beautifully, never once flinching at words like "autistic" or "pervasive." It's natural to feel overwhelmed at the beginning, but necessary to get past that feeling and move toward a more constructive emotion: pride.

We have every right to be proud of our children, perhaps more than parents of neurotypical children do. And we should make sure we communicate that to our children, not only in words, but in the way we act and the way we treat their disorder. If we behave as if we think there is something to hide, something of which we should be ashamed or be embarrassed by, our children – Asperger Syndrome or not – will pick up on that, and the message we'll be sending is exactly the one we least wish to send: there's something wrong with you, and it's something we don't want anyone else to know about.

However, most Asperger parents find it possible to progress beyond that, and even if they don't become advocates for children with autism spectrum disorders, they can at least exude an aura of confidence and pride in their children's accomplishments.

Yesterday, Josh came home from school complaining mildly about the number of small projects his teachers had assigned toward the end of the school year. Then he brightened. "But I don't have to worry about when they're due, because it says in my IEP that I can hand things in a day or two late," he said. This was news to me, because I don't recall that being written into his IEP. I also hadn't known Josh was aware he *had* an IEP.

I told him in no uncertain terms that he was to get those projects done on time. "That is written in there for the times that you're not able to do the work on time because of your Asperger Syndrome," I told him. "You're perfectly capable of getting this done on time, and that's exactly what you're going to do."

Explaining that to him, even though it made him grumble, should communicate to Josh that I expect him to do his best academically, and that I don't ever consider him to be less than adequate to the tasks he's given. There is no reason his AS should impact on his studies at this level, he's gotten perfectly good grades, and he can't hide behind his disorder to try and catch a break. I like to think he's getting a measure of my pride from that, because I am proud that he can be a very good student without letting his AS get in the way. More likely, he thinks I am a mean old taskmaster who doesn't see how nicely he could have sidestepped the system and still gotten a good grade.

Those who hold our hands and pity us are missing the point. They look at our children and see a disability, whereas we look at the disability and see our children. We know the full range of ability, the possibilities our kids have that may fly under the radar of the casual observer. We know the complete individuals they are, Asperger Syndrome or no. And so the education, the raising of the awareness level in general society, must begin with us. Nobody else is going to do it.

Begin, obviously, with those you know the best, but if you feel the urge, educate on the local level. Organize an evening with other Asperger parents in your town and stage a talk at the local library (you can use this book as a jumping-off point, if you like). Write articles for the local newspaper. Find out what the local autism organization is and raise both funds and consciousness with a movie night (maybe not *Rain Man*) or a garage sale – whatever is best for your temperament and your area. But make the issue local, and visible. Make sure people in your town, your city, your county can't easily avoid finding out more about Asperger Syndrome and autism spectrum disorders in general.

Work with the local school district (it can't hurt to educate the teachers and administrators who are working with more autism spectrum students than ever before). Hold an evening with the PTA to educate other parents and school staff at the same time. Invite officers from a nearby support group to speak.

All of these things can be done with little or no money. They might not have the impact of a full-blown feature on a network news program (or, as I like to flatter myself, a feature in a Sunday newspaper supplement), but they will work toward raising the level of awareness about Asperger Syndrome, and that should be the immediate goal of anyone who knows someone with AS.

"We're fairly disorganized," says Dennis Debbaudt, law enforcement advocate and educator for autism spectrum disorders. According to Debbaudt, the autism community has not reached the same level as organizations that represent other disabilities, and therefore isn't as well understood or as well represented. "The state of the autism advocacy community is fairly sad and it's not getting any better. It's pretty sad out there. That's one of the reasons that we're the last ones to the table."

At the "grass-roots" level, you and I can help by bridging the gap. We can remember every time someone looked pityingly at us and decide to turn our annoyance into constructive action. We can take our children's special interests and make them work for them: if your child is especially focused on baseball statistics, get in touch with your nearest minor or major league team, and see if an "Asperger Syndrome Night" can be organized. Suggest that it be publicized on the team's radio and television broadcasts and provide copy for the announcers to read that explains (as briefly as possible) what AS is, and what needs to be done.

In short, become a publicity machine. My friend Michael Levine, the top-notch Hollywood publicist (Michael has worked with Michael Jackson, Barbra Streisand, Michael J. Fox and Charlton Heston, among countless others), wrote a book called *Guerrilla P.R.*, which has become the undisputed bible of publicity for those on a budget (that is, it was undisputed until Michael himself wrote a sequel, *Guerrilla P.R. Wired*, which explores possibilities for those who would like to draw attention to themselves using the Internet). In it, Michael discusses ways to raise the awareness of a business, a person or an organization through generating publicity.

Among other things, he suggests finding newsworthy aspects of your message, targeting local media, sending out press releases and forging relationships with local editors, reporters and news producers. Michael's audience is mostly made up of businesspeople hoping to publicize their products and services, but it doesn't have to be limited to that by any stretch of the imagination.

The same principles can be used just as effectively in making the public more aware of Asperger Syndrome and autism spectrum disorders. Write press releases. Stage events. Get explanations of the disorder into local newspapers, on cable TV talk shows, on the local news and other fact-based radio and television broadcasts. Keep the name in the news, and explain as much as you can without overloading the media. Find ways to keep the message interesting to the general public and keep reinventing the message itself. Don't let the current deplorable state of awareness remain un-raised.

Don't misunderstand, nobody expects every Asperger parent to become a dynamo of self-promotion. We don't think you should expose yourself and your child to media scrutiny strictly in the service of The Cause. After all, even as I was writing about Josh in a national magazine, I made darn sure his face was not in the photographs. There is no requirement for self-declaration. Do what you feel comfortable doing.

The Mope can become a motivating factor instead of a symbol of everything you don't want your child's life to become. It can spur your forward. You don't have to devote your life to the cause of autism spectrum disorders and their woeful underrepresentation in our society's consciousness. There's no need to feel inadequate if you don't become the next advocate for Asperger Syndrome in your state. But do what you can. Each tiny step makes a difference; it is that much less that will still need to be done.

After all, it was The Mope that got me started writing this book.

I Am NOT the Butler Around Here

*I*T'S THE PHRASE I HEAR IN MY SLEEP, the one that I repeat so many times in the course of a day that I'm thinking of having it engraved on my business cards. I say it exclusively to Josh, since he seems to be the only one who hasn't absorbed the information contained in it yet. And as the day wears on, I seem to say it with an increasing level of volume:

I am NOT the butler around here!

I have uttered that phrase in jest; I have snarled it, spat it, screamed it, raged it, tossed it off, sighed it and moaned it. It has escaped my lips before I had a chance to recognize it, and at other times, I have built up to it like the high note in an aria. I believe that if the phone rings at two o'clock in the morning, my first words will be, "I am NOT the butler around here. Hello?"

In my heart, I know that Josh doesn't *mean* to sound like I'm his faithful employee and should simply do whatever he suggests.

173

I know that when he says, "Where's dinner?" he actually means, "Excuse me, Dad. When will dinner be ready?" And I know that virtually every other parent of a twelve-year-old, Asperger Syndrome or not, will hear roughly the same thing on occasion.

But I also know that Asperger Syndrome makes it more difficult for my son to understand that his tone of voice and the turn of phrase he chooses can give his words a meaning that he might not have intended. Because he doesn't understand that fact, and can't recognize it when it happens, he uses that tone of voice and turn that phrase much more often than a neurotypical child, and after a good number of repetitions, even the most patient father on earth – whom I am not – would be reaching the end of his rope.

It generally goes like this. I'm on deadline for an article that's due today, and the afternoon is starting to wear on toward evening. Behind me, there is stomping on the stairs, and Josh appears to my right, his voice preceding him into the room.

"Um, Dad?"

"Um, Josh, don't you see I'm working? What if I were on the phone?" There is a long pause, during which he does not reply. "Okay, what do you want?"

"Um, I have a problem."

I moan, hopefully inwardly. "What does that mean, Josh?"

"Um, the cord came out of my computer and fell behind my desk."

"Don't say 'um' all the time, okay? So get the cord and put it back in. Didn't this just happen yesterday, too? What are you doing to that computer?"

"Nothing! I'm doing nothing! It just comes out! Why don't you believe me?"

This is a common refrain, and its repetition doesn't calm me down. "I didn't say I don't believe you, Josh. Now, you've told me your problem. What do you want?"

"I *want* you to come up and fix my computer!"

"Joshua, watch your tone. *I am NOT the butler around here!*"

See how that works? By the time this conversation is over, I will have stomped up the stairs ahead of him, complaining that nobody around this house can ever seem to take care of a problem besides me, and he will be complaining behind me that I never believe him when he tells me something's wrong. I will reach under his desk, pull out the power cord from his desk, mumbling the whole time, and connect it to his computer. Finally, we will part company on less than spectacular terms.

Just to see how many ways I can be a bad parent in the course of one conversation, let's analyze exactly what went wrong here, step by step.

First, I have left the most difficult part of my workday until very close to my deadline, which means I'm going to be more on edge than otherwise, and will have less time to deal with my children's problems. Asperger parents who work at home should note that it's better to get your work done when your children are not at home, whenever possible. But this obstacle could easily have been overcome, and wasn't a major contributing factor.

Josh stomps down the stairs. He's not irritated yet; he just stomps wherever he goes. He approaches me and starts talking before he enters the room. This irritates me because he also does it when I'm conducting telephone interviews, and he hasn't checked to see that I'm not on the phone now. So already, I'm annoyed.

Here's where I make the first in a series of similar mistakes: I try to attack each issue as it happens, rather than focusing on the main problem, which will turn out to be that his tone of voice has me feeling like a servant, the Pet Peeve. Before I even find out what the problem is, I'm criticizing him on his habit of talking before he has viewed and assessed the situation. I snap at him about not talking on the way into the room, and he is already on edge, knowing that he wants something from me and that I'm irritated, and this isn't going the way he wants it to.

175

Rule #1: Focus on the one issue you really want to address, and don't sweat the small stuff.

"Um, I have a problem."

Here, I distract both of us with a side issue. Is this *really* the time to worry about whether he says "um" before each sentence? Probably not. If I weren't on deadline, I might have let that one go by, but I'm distracted. Not to mention, my simply repeating his "um" sarcastically and not addressing the issue head-on will either: (a) go right over his head with no chance of an impact or (b) tick him off.

He also hears me sigh, and if I'm not careful, he sees me roll my eyes. I'm sending my son signals that he's bothering me, when in his mind, he has a perfectly legitimate problem that his father should, indeed, help him with.

Rule #2: Try to present a cheerful front. If you show irritation before you have a strong reason to do so, you're going to get nervousness in return. This will not help.

"What does that mean, Josh?"

I know perfectly well what "I have a problem" means. It means he wants me to do something for him. But I want Josh to ask politely for help, given the dozens of times we have played this scenario out in the past. I'd like to believe there's a chance he's absorbed the problem by now. But I should be able to tell by his demeanor that he hasn't, and this is going to be another in a series of Pet Peeve situations.

Rule #3: This is the moment to brace yourself. You obviously know what's coming, and you should be planning your response, which should be a calm and considered one.

"Um, the cord came out of my computer and fell behind my desk."

Immediately, reread rule #1. This is even less the time to deal with the "um" problem. And my suggestion that he go fix his own problem should also be shot out the window, because this is hardly the first time we've had this discussion, and I know he's afraid to deal with electrical cords. Except in those cases when he thinks it's fun, in which case he won't tell me he's plugged and unplugged something fifty times.

Rule #4: Think about your own responses before you respond. If you can predict the outcome, and it isn't what you're trying to achieve, don't use that response.

"Didn't this just happen yesterday, too? What are you doing to that computer?"

Sometimes I wonder which one of us has more difficulty learning. Sure, this was something that happened yesterday. Absolutely, it's a recurring problem. Maybe he's even doing something while working on the computer that makes the cord fall out. But is this the time to distract him, yet again, with another issue? Particularly when *my* tone is the one that's causing the problem now, sounding more accusatory than it meant to be?

Rule #5: Don't expect your child to learn by example if your example is as bad as his behavior.

Naturally, here is where Josh blows up about my insinuation that he is the cause of the problem. His quick fuse (I've often wondered where he picked up such a trait) burns to the end and he retaliates, confronting me on my accusation and changing the conversation to be about a Pet Peeve of his own, his belief that his parents don't find him trustworthy. This, from a boy who lies about washing his hair.

I come back with a defensive statement about believing him (despite evidence to the contrary) and decide to force the issue: "What do you want?" This tactic, which could work if it hadn't been preceded by all the animosity, is just begging for the response it is about to get.

Rule #6: Don't set your child up to fail in a conversation.

"I *want* you to come up and fix my computer!"

There it is, the tone I've been waiting for. Part of my irritation here is exacerbated by the fact that he used the phrase "come up and fix," which plays into the fact that my resistance has been based, at least a little bit, on my reluctance to stand up and haul my weary butt up the stairs.

Rule #7: Gauge your own mood. If you're weary or anxious, you're not likely to respond as calmly as you should. Give yourself more time to respond in these situations.

"Joshua, watch your tone. *I am NOT the butler around here!*"

And there it is: the Pet Peeve, carefully nurtured by both parties, has been let out of its box. Now it's my turn to stomp up the stairs and act like a six-year-old. The difference is that he's a lot closer to six than I am, and I should know better.

Rule #8: Pet Peeves don't need any help. Let them happen naturally; don't invite them to come out and play.

Having reread this section, I will now leave my desk for a few minutes and sit quietly with my eyes closed. Self-criticism is a humbling business.

Okay, I'm back: Each Asperger parent has one trait, one particular hot button, that especially irritates his or her sensibilities. For some, it is the child's obsessive devotion to a special interest, to the exclusion of any other topic of conversation. Others are especially disturbed by food issues, difficulties with peers, a seeming lack of empathy for others, unusually immature behavior in view of the child's chronological age, and so on. Usually, the "hot button" issue is very specific – the way the child can't keep his hands still, the "stimming" given any provocation at all, the unusual phrasing of speech, or the child's inability to tie her shoes at age nine.

We are not discussing a rational emotion here; we understand that our children's behavior is in some way governed by their AS. But we react instinctively, sure that if we just explain it *one more time*, we can reach the child and solve the problem.

We can't.

Yes, repetition of an idea can sometimes penetrate the interference between our children's heads and the rest of the world; and yes, we have to keep trying to get through no matter what, but in the case of our Pet Peeve, that one hot button, our patience is going to be especially thin. The question becomes whether we can restrain ourselves long enough to get out of the room before a pitched screaming argument begins, not whether we can find a way to achieve our goal in this area.

The key, as it was with other adults who might make insensitive remarks, is the Cleansing Breath.

This concept, which was the one and only thing I took away from the natural childbirth classes, watching while my wife did all the hard work, is that deep, deep breath that not only fills our lungs with oxygen, but also provides a good stretch of seconds when we can compose ourselves, get the red field out of our mind's eyes, and prepare to deal with the stimulus with which we've just been presented.

It's an easy concept to understand, but a difficult technique to master. Because Asperger Syndrome is having its way with us, we need to spot the times when a Cleansing Breath is necessary, and learn to take the moment and use it. It is the exact equivalent of the "count to ten" method people used to employ to calm themselves during a stressful moment when acting on impulse would most likely be unfortunate.

The thing is, telling someone to calm down is as useful as explaining to a child with Asperger Syndrome that the schedule of the northeast corridor line of the New Jersey Transit System is not necessarily the most fascinating topic of conversation available on the planet. You can intend to do it, but it might not do as much good as you'd like.

There is no special "trick" to learning how (or more specifically, when) to insert the Cleansing Breath into your dealings with your child. Sometimes a physical cue (tightly clenched jaw, fists balling up, biting your lip) can alert you to the need for a pause. But sometimes, you won't notice that cue until you've already blown your stack. In other instances, the situation might allow you to notice that you're about to "go off," but won't suggest an alternative behavior while you're still angry.

You have to know your own pattern. When your personal Pet Peeve scenario begins to play itself out, try to notice the first signs. In the example above, I probably knew that Josh would end up saying something that would make me feel like his employee, and if I'd thought about it, I could either have preempted the incident, or corrected him without losing my cool. Sometimes even I manage to do that. Not always, but sometimes.

Catch yourself before the scene plays out too far, and warn yourself that this often doesn't end well. If you're more aware of each reaction as you go along, and you pay attention to your own feelings, rather than trying to make every correction your child needs all at the same time, you'll have a much better outcome in most cases.

Nevertheless, you'll never be perfect; get used to that now. I still hear myself saying, "I am NOT the butler around here" more than I would like (I'd like not to say it at all). And in researching for and writing this book, I have found more than enough reasons to empathize with my son, to realize that most of the time his intentions are *not* to annoy or irritate, but simply to communicate, and that he is clumsy with his communication tools in ways that a neurotypical child might not be. He is a neurotypical twelve-year-old, squared. And the problems are often more in my reactions than his actions. So I work with tempering myself. You might understand; it's not an easy thing to do.

Still, there is a happy ending of sorts to this story. In the past few years, Josh and I have grown up together. He has learned which conversational tones and phrases are likely to push people's buttons (not just mine, I hasten to note), and I have learned to listen for what he *means* rather than what he *says*. We are a work in progress.

These days, Josh is less likely to ask someone (usually me or his mother) to get him an apple when he's perfectly capable of doing it himself. He doesn't always take pride in being able to accomplish household tasks, the way he did when he would learn a new skill at age eight. But he understands that he is a member of a family, not, as my wife would call him, "the pasha," who would have his needs attended to by the loyal staff.

That's the trend, anyway. Day-to-day living provides more of a one-step-forward-two-steps-back approach for the Asperger parent, but the progress that is accomplished, however slow and painful, is still progress. Sometimes you have to think back a year or two and imagine how your child would have reacted to a situation then. In comparing it to his reaction now, you will find that the hard work he and you have done is paying off.

Asperger parents live in that progress; we find our solace and our pride in the smaller accomplishments our children manage, and thrill to the larger ones we know others don't even notice. A lot of that progress comes when we, ourselves, manage to learn a new skill – the ability to take a Cleansing Breath and pause a moment before we react. It's a skill we might have to acquire later in life than we should have, but one that is immeasurably helpful in dealing with the particular set of circumstances we have to face every day.

Sure, it's the kind of thing every parent of any child will understand. Absolutely, the parents of neurotypical children have to pick up socks left on the floor, explain the same rule of the house for the umpteenth time to a child watching television and only half-listening. They have to deal with temper tantrums (ones that we would barely notice, but tantrums nonetheless). They must look forward to the same adolescent posturing and attitude that we dread. And they, too, can benefit from the Cleansing Breath.

But like everything else, the Pet Peeve is a question not of frequency, but of *degree* and *intensity*, and that is why parents of neurotypical children don't understand our reactions. They think our children are "going through a phase" or are "highstrung." Some of them think that our children are the best behaved people on the planet, and that we are insane. It doesn't matter.

We know the roadblocks in our children's paths. We know that we're supposed to help them avoid the pitfalls and grow confidence, self-esteem and social skills. And we know that there will be days, or parts of days, when we're too weary to do all the things we should do and take the Cleansing Breaths we need to take. We know we're not always going to succeed in calming ourselves when the Pet Peeve rears its ugly head. But if we can improve our batting averages overall, that is at least a start in the right direction. And maybe we can even get our children to help us along the path.

After all, we're not the butlers around here.

Adolescence Is Coming – I'm Getting an Apartment

*L*ORI SHERY SAYS IT BEST: "NOW THAT Adam is a teenager, we have our share of yelling matches. I'll tell him, 'If you don't like it, find another mother.' And he'll say, 'Fine, I'll find a better one.' I'll say, 'You know where your bags are.' And he'll say, 'I can't pack them fast enough.' And then I think: this is adolescence."

As I write this, Joshua is twelve years old, and will be a sixth-grader for another three days. By the time this book is published, he will have entered middle school, and will be a teenager. It tightens my stomach just to type those words.

The teenage years of middle school and high school are difficult enough for a child who doesn't have a neurological disorder. It is a time of cliques and social strata, a time when children who did not pass judgment on each other for their first twelve years begin to change alliances, form new friendships, end old ones and decide, with very little in terms of criteria, who is "cool" and who is not.

Add Asperger Syndrome to the equation, and you have a highly volatile situation.

"They get depressed and anxious," says Dr. Elizabeth Roberts. "They're at a much higher risk than 'normal' kids for depression and anxiety, because as they hit adolescence, they become more aware. They're being rejected, and they want to go out with girls, and the girls think they're weird. That's when we start diagnosing depression and medicating for depression. I would bet that their suicide rate is higher than the unaffected population but probably not as high as other psychiatric groups, but I have not seen any statistics on that."

Children with AS, whose social skills have always been a challenge, enter their teens at a disadvantage. And the last thing they need at a time when social interaction is intensifying is a disadvantage.

"The middle school and beginning high school years, that time period, are very cliquish and kids are very concerned with popularity and whether they will fit in, for a variety of reasons," says Dr. Jed Baker. "One is that their environment changes. There's a new school, and kids coming from different schools, so they have to see if they're going to fit in. Just developmentally, it's a time when kids begin to question again who they are, if they're likable, lovable, attractive, interesting, because their bodies are changing and cognitively they're developing. They start to be aware of things they weren't aware of before. People's personalities become much more prevalent (as a reason for friendship) than whether this person lives next to you. Friendships are chosen not because you live next door or you got the same toy, but because of what people are characterologically like. They have better abstract thinking, so they're not just looking at physical characteristics, they're looking at what people's traits are. To me, it's like the game *Survivor*. You get voted out. You go through a series of challenges and at the end they kick somebody out. That's what middle school lunchroom is essentially like. You go through certain challenges during the day, and all of a sudden someone's kicked out and he or she doesn't know why. Your best friend yesterday is now hooked up with some group and you're out."

It's tough for any teenager. For teens with AS, there are points that make it more and less challenging than for their neurotypical peers. People on the autism spectrum are likely to have quirks and personality traits that will make them seem unusual to others, and that will intensify during the teenage years. On the other hand, a teen's AS might make him more withdrawn to begin with, and he might not be as hard hit by the judgment of his peers as he "flies under the radar." That's not much of a blessing, but it may be a helpful truth in some cases.

As with any other time in their development, teens with AS will inevitably react to stimuli in the same way as their neurotypical peers, only more intensely. So the usual bouts of reticent behavior, rebellion, self-absorption and surliness will come home with a teen with AS, more obvious and louder than they might in the typical home.

It's only a few months away, and I'm already scouting around town for an apartment for the next seven years. Not for Josh; for me. I think the only logical solution is to hide.

Okay, so maybe that's not the most serious statement I've ever made. Maybe it is possible to live with a teenager who has Asperger Syndrome and survive with your sanity intact. Maybe, indeed, it is possible to enjoy these years with your child.

Consider that Asperger parents are among the very few who can rejoice at the signs of rebellion and petulance in their teens – they are indications that the child is developing along the lines of his neurotypical peers. "Every time he does something adolescent, first it's annoyance but then it's: he's doing something normal, thank God," says Lori Shery of ASPEN. "With Adam now, I tell him 'do this' and he's like, 'make me.' Obviously I don't like to hear that, but you know what, that's normal stuff and it's OK. And I know he won't be an adolescent forever because otherwise I'd be totally gray."

Getting through these difficult years has never been a picnic; very few people remember their teenage years with great fondness. But I remind myself that the pre-teen years are not supposed to be easy, and that Josh's behavior has actually improved the past three or four years. Where there was once physically aggressive acting out, there is now verbal acting out, which is an improvement. The middle and high school years don't have to be terrible.

You're probably as tired of reading these words as I am of typing them, but the truth is that *preparation is the key to any aspect of Asperger Syndrome.* Knowing what to expect, and making sure your child knows what to expect, can make an enormous difference in the way you each treat the teenage years, and the communication that can (really!) flow between you while it's all going on.

Yes, it's true that adolescents are more prone to depression and anxiety than young children, and that there are dangers associated with both these conditions. It's true that our children are just as susceptible to both these dangers as neurotypical children, if not more so. But if we know – and our children know – the warning signs, we can recognize and deal with problems as they arise, rather than waiting until situations are out of control.

I think it's appropriate to emphasize once again that I am not a psychologist, nor an expert in neurological disorders. I'm a parent, like you are. I have spoken to other parents, to psychologists and neurologists, and I have done research about the condition we all face. But I am no expert. Don't do one single thing you read about in this book unless you think it makes sense, and if it is a medical or psychological point, consult a trained professional before you even consider taking any advice you read here. Remember, this book is your carry-on support group, not your doctor-to-go.

With that said, let's examine what some warning signs for depression in adolescents can be, so we will be ready if they show up in our children. Remember that it's normal to be sad periodically, especially if things are going wrong in our lives, and that teenagers are given to mood swings. It's prolonged dark moods that should concern us.

Psychologists say that major changes in an adolescent's mood or habits can be a signal of depression. Precipitously dropping grades at school, for example, or sudden indifference to things that held great interest before can be signs that something other than a normal teenage funk is brewing. As with anything else, the best way to battle such things is to keep open lines of communication between parent and teenager, although that's often easier said than done.

During the adolescent years, tension between parents and children often heightens. This is no place to debate the various psychological reasons proposed for this phenomenon; each case is different, anyway. But nobody who has ever lived with or been a teenager will dispute that there is usually an increased level of friction.

For an Asperger parent, an increased level of friction with a child already given to mood swings is not a pleasant prospect. But we have a weapon that most parents whose children are entering adolescence don't: we've been dealing with children on the autism spectrum for thirteen years. What's coming may be more intense than what we're used to, but it won't be anything new.

We know that our children will sometimes act petulant and moody; we know they'll burst into angry tears or screams with what seems to be little or no provocation. We've had loud, intense arguments with our children that even we didn't understand. We've seen tantrums and meltdowns, endured the cold shoulder, sat through tense family dinners, waited for the next explosion and had epithets flung at us by the people we love the most in this world.

Been there, done that!

Asperger parents have already devised strategies for dealing with difficult times, and have executed them, found which ones were effective and which ones were not. We have more knowledge of the way our children's minds work than most parents, because we have *needed* to learn more. We are virtual experts on the ins and outs of each of our children.

Now, that doesn't mean it's all going to be easy. In fact, it doesn't mean *any* part of the coming years is going to be easy. With older children come more adult, deeper problems, ones that can't be overcome with a tickle, a chocolate bar or a trip to the park. Adolescents have to deal with adult problems, without the benefit of ever having been an adult. In the six years that cover most school systems' middle and high schools, most teens will be dealing with increased peer interaction, more exclusive socialization (more cliques, fewer kids who "understand"), the possibilities of drug and alcohol abuse, increased academic pressure and less structured schedules. And they'll have to do all that while their bodies are leading them insistently toward (brace yourself) *sex*.

Interaction between the genders increases during the teenage years, and becomes more complicated by geometric degrees. There are many things about our children that are different than with their neurotypical peers, but their physical development isn't one of them. Hormones flow just as rapidly in a teenager with Asperger Syndrome as in one who doesn't have AS, and they are just as difficult to ignore. The problem is that impulse control has never been a strong feature of the Asperger Syndrome makeup, and during the teenage years, a child with AS is feeling more, and different, impulses than ever before.

This can lead to very difficult situations. Social strata in middle and high school are often delineated through romantic relationships, so teens with AS, who are less likely to have girlfriends or boyfriends, already have one strike against them – one that will be compounded by the seemingly odd behavior, stimming and other "differences" that have been present since the child entered kindergarten. This scenario can lead to frustration on the part of the teen with AS, and frustration during the teenage years, when boys especially are bigger and stronger than they used to be, can be a dangerous emotion.

After all, neurotypical teenagers are frustrated much of the time, and many of them act out in inappropriate ways. But a teen with Asperger Syndrome, who might have a history of acting out, will often compound the problem with over-the-top responses to stimuli. Teenagers have an abundance of stimuli.

One of the more consistent quirks of people with Asperger Syndrome is that they don't take well to subtlety; they "don't know when to quit." When a teen's body is telling him one thing and the person he's with is trying to be diplomatic about telling him another, misunderstandings are almost inevitable.

Parents who had trouble with the "birds and the bees" speech with their children who have Asperger Syndrome are going to find it more difficult to be explicit and clear about the intricacies of romantic and physical relationships, but they don't have a choice. Teenagers with AS *must* be given all the information they need, and sooner is much better than later. Sending a teen with Asperger Syndrome to high school without explaining some of the social problems he's about to face is like sending him into battle with a feather. It's better than nothing, but not much.

Dennis Debbaudt, who educates law enforcement officers about the autism spectrum, emphasizes that it's not possible to give our teens too much information about interpersonal relationships. When people on the spectrum don't understand, and become infatuated, their feelings can be overwhelming, and the gentle rebuffs of those who don't understand can be badly misunderstood.

"We don't tell our kids enough about anything, to be general," Debbaudt says. "They need us not to pull punches for them, to tell them what can happen and what the consequences will be if they don't behave the way they're expected to behave. Protecting them from life isn't going to work."

What that means – and it doesn't matter how uncomfortable you are with such subjects – is that you have to discuss sex with your child on a semi-regular basis, and to explain not only about abstinence, if that's your wish for your child, but also about how to be safe if something of an intimate nature does happen for him or her. This is not a time to be delicate; discuss condoms and make sure the teenager knows where to get them and to have them available if any possibility of a sexual encounter is present.

Make it your business to know who your teenager's friends are, and whether any of them are involved in sexual relationships. We may flatter ourselves and believe we are still our children's primary role models, but these are the years when they start to pay more attention to their peers, and even if the words "everybody's doing it" aren't spoken, they will be part of the conversation. Ask questions, and get answers without being judgmental or insistent. Be understanding and open. And keep in mind, I'm not saying any of this will be easy.

The same principle is important when dealing with the topic of substance abuse. The most serious peer pressure about drugs and alcohol comes during the middle and high school years, and while some of our children are not very susceptible to peer pressure (they don't notice what the other kids are doing), others are only too aware of their differences and eager to do what they can to "fit in." For some of our kids, the temptation to seem "one of the gang" is stronger than the training they've received about staying away from dangerous substances.

Again, preparation is key. We can only warn our children so much, but we can explain exactly how the temptation will manifest itself, and the reasons we want them to respond in one way, and not another. But that's not enough.

Asperger parents are used to being attuned to every nuance of their children's moods, so remaining vigilant and observant through the teenage years is not that much of a change. However, the teen with AS is probably going to be more concerned with his privacy than ever before, and will almost certainly not be as forthcoming about his day, his feelings and even the people he's involved with as he was at age ten or eleven.

That doesn't mean we should throw up our hands and do nothing. We need to be meticulous about our children's moods when they reach these years, and try to hold our tempers in check more stringently. A teenager who isn't challenged and opposed at every turn is more likely to communicate with his parents than one who feels he won't be heard and considered if he does speak.

Try to remember how you felt as a teenager (no matter how ancient that era might now seem, even to you). Your parents were a constant source of embarrassment; your friends were the only ones who really knew what was going on, and you had to keep them from finding out that you didn't know anything about anything. The knowledge that everybody felt like that, and was making it up as they went along, would come much later, when it was no longer of any use.

No matter how hard you try, the odds are you won't be your teenager's best friend. But Asperger Syndrome adds to the feelings of alienation that most teens go through, since in your teen's case he really *is* different, and he knows it. So try your best to be open on those rare occasions when he does want to talk, and don't react with shock or embarrassment when subjects you're not used to discussing crop up. In fact, raise those subjects yourself, to be sure that you do discuss them at some time or another.

Given all that, you have to try to remain on an even keel. There will be times when your teen will push the art of being obnoxious to new heights, and you won't always be able to hold your temper down against an onslaught of insults, abuse and sneers (these come with the territory of all teenagers' parents). You will occasionally snap. You will give as good as you get. You will find yourself wondering later exactly what you were thinking about when you said *that*. And you will wonder how your child, whom you brought up from the tiniest baby, could possibly have thought to say that to *you*.

The message remains the same: try not to let that happen, but when it does, don't let it set you back too far. Forgive yourself for being human, and move on. Consider the fights you had with *your* parents, and remember that they, in all likelihood, still loved you when the argument was over, and you, if you absolutely had to admit it, still loved them. Those truths remain to this day in your own family. Don't cross the line so far that it can't be uncrossed, and you will live to be driven crazy by a teenager another day.

Nobody ever said the teenage years were easy, but at least you've had thirteen years to prepare for them. And as an Asperger parent, you know that preparation is everything.

Summertime, and the Living Is ... Impossible

*W*HEN THE SCHOOL BELL RINGS ON the last day of class, neurotypical children let out a cry of jubilation. Children with Asperger Syndrome are just as likely to emit a groan of foreboding.

It's not that kids with AS love school so much that they can't bear the thought of leaving. Children who have autism spectrum disorders are extremely reliant on the ritual of routine, their safe, sure structured day. Summer offers anything but structure, and the thought of all that free time, without a carefully considered plan in place, can be unnerving.

If you were asked to do your job, which you've been doing for months, in a new office, with none of the tools or plans you're used to relying upon, you might feel a little out of sorts, too. For a child with Asperger Syndrome, who has had to learn something

193

as simple and basic as what a frown means, the lack of familiar structure is an untested, worrisome thing to face.

The ten (or so) weeks between the stressful last day of the school year and the stressful first day of the next school year can be even more nerve-wracking than winter vacation or spring break. For an Asperger parent, decision making about summer has to begin months before final report cards are being issued, during a time when the weather might be freezing and other parents might give an odd look to someone who mentions the possibility of day camp in July and August.

For those who work outside the home (and for some of us, like we freelance writers, who work inside the home), day camp, sleep-away camp or some other organized program might be the answer to the Summertime Asperger Blues. For others, day trips and the inevitable strains of "I'm bored" are more in tune. Camp, no matter how it is presented, is not inexpensive, and opens a number of questions, including the same one you faced about school: inclusion, or special needs?

As I've mentioned, for Josh, we decided, after a not terribly successful stint in a typical camp, on a special needs day camp called Harbor Haven, which is about an hour from our house, in West Orange, New Jersey. Much like during the school year, Josh gets up around seven, and gets himself ready to leave the house by eight. Unlike during the school year, however, a van comes to pick him up and take him to the camp, where he spends the day with other children with mild to moderate disabilities, all falling into the neurological categories of ADD, ADHD, PDD-NOS, Asperger Syndrome, other autism spectrum disorders, and so on.

We decided on the camp because of the experience Josh had in the "mainstream" day camp, and because he needed a place where he could go every day for seven weeks and not be "the unusual kid." This was an individual choice, specific to Josh, and might not be what your child needs. Some children do well in camp with neurotypical children on their own; others go with an aide, like during the school year. For us, the best solution was

Harbor Haven, and Josh is (as I write this) about to start his fourth summer there.

Robyn Tanne, director of Harbor Haven, says many parents bring their children to the camp after having a less than satisfactory experience with a typical day camp setting. "Probably about fifty percent of the families or closer to sixty, have tried some other form of summer programming in a typical setting," she says. "Usually it was unsuccessful. Camp is harder for kids to be mainstreamed into because the primary thing that you're promoting there is the social interaction. It's about friendships, it's about conversation with your peers; you're not quiet in camp. You're talking all the time. When you're walking to activities, you're not walking in lines through the hallway quietly. If you're in a typical camp setting, and all the boys are talking about Pokémon or cars or the ballgame that was on that night, our kids have no interest, not to mention knowledge, and can care less about that. They're going to be the odd person out. The more they're left out, the worse the summer is going to go."

She adds: "In a typical camp setting, you usually have high school or college students as counselors. They do not know how to help facilitate, whereas in a school setting, when your child is included in a class, you're dealing with professionals. Those professionals are going to try and help. It's also about academics in school. A lot of our kids are great academically. They can show off, even they can excel in some areas. But in camp, it's all social; it's all recreational type activities. In typical care settings, it's also very competitive once you get into certain age groups. It can be very cliquish, and there's a very little tolerance for difference. In the schools, they have to be very tolerant of differences. The people are more trained. I always like to say, you can't use the inclusion environment in an academic setting necessarily as a gauge for how your child is going to do in summer camp. Summer camp is much harder."

Some Asperger parents organize their work schedules to avoid summer camp entirely, but that's not possible for all of us.

And while some older children with AS can handle a residential camp, where children stay for two months without coming home, many are not capable of separating from their families for that long, or would be horrified by such a drastic change in routine, even at a camp designed to their special needs.

Lori Shery's son Adam, for example, went to a camp in the Poconos for a few weeks during the past few summers, and while she reports there were some hiccups, overall the experience was a positive one. "He made it through," Lori says. "It was a very big step for Adam, and for us."

At a day camp that accommodates special needs, the "drop-off" in academics that sometimes follows a long summer can be lessened or avoided, as there are brief academic periods during a day of swimming, crafts, nature, games and sports (although noncompetitive sports). Typical-setting camps can also sometimes accommodate special needs through a process that resembles the IEP development that goes on in schools. Either a special counselor or an outside aide, hired by the parents, can help some children with AS through a more typical camp summer.

Again, for Josh, Harbor Haven has been a very positive experience. Robyn Tanne says the camp's mission is to provide the kind of environment in which our children can find friends and activities they enjoy, but without the cut-throat competition that some day camps can encourage, and with the special supports, like special education-trained staff and social skills workshops, that our children need.

Some parents believe, as my wife and I do with Josh, that their children work hard enough to make it through the school year, and need to relax during the summer in a place where the same kind of pressure to "fit in" that increases as our children get older doesn't exist in as severe an environment.

"A lot of parents think that their kids feel such stress to be in that included world and to make it work that they do want them to relax," Robyn says. "A lot of parents want their kids to feel like they're the top of the heap for a change, to let their guard down. It's not like we want all their bad behaviors to all come out in the summertime. But they can let their guard down so that if they slip up, we're able to deal with it. We're able to bring them back on track. A lot of parents also want the promotion of the social aspect of camp, and they don't believe their children are going to get that in an included, typical camp setting. We have social skills groups; we have our crisis intervention person who's going to work with the kids if they have a moment. If our kids lose it – which they are very likely to do in (a typical camp) setting – they're going to get kicked out."

Asperger parents looking for a special needs camp that caters specifically to AS and other autism spectrum disorders might check with local support groups, or the Asperger Syndrome web sites www.aspenjn.org, www.asperger.org, and www.udel.edu/bkirby/asperger, among others. There might be suggestions, or at least hints, there.

Camp fairs are often held in the winter, and many local day camps will have exhibits there. Seek them out (newspaper weekend sections list them, and they may advertise) and attend; there won't be many special needs camps represented, but you only need one that understands your child.

The key component is *understanding*. The camp that truly has a background in AS and comprehends the accommodations that must be made and *why* they are necessary is the one that can best help your child have an enjoyable, productive summer. Children with social skills problems might even make some new friends.

One of Josh's closest friends is a boy he met at Harbor Haven three years ago, who now comes to our home periodically for sleepovers, and who invites Josh to his house to "hang around." Because they share certain traits of AS, they communicate on a level that Josh can't always achieve with neurotypical peers. They don't have to explain as much, and they completely understand each other's quirks.

Robyn Tanne attributes much of the success of any special needs camp to the experience level of the staff. Those who have worked in special education environments before and have a working knowledge of Asperger Syndrome are naturally more likely to recognize difficult situations and be able to handle them smoothly.

The staff at Harbor Haven is trained for about twenty-five hours, including five during the summer, when the counselors and staff know the children better and can address specific issues. This is in addition to any previous experience the counselors, teachers and staff might have had before starting at Harbor Haven.

There are, of course, many other day camps and sleep-away camps that cater to children with special needs. Children whose disorder affects them more severely might not be able to thrive in an environment like Harbor Haven, and might not be accepted to the camp if the director thinks the camp can't accommodate their needs. Since most children with AS tend to be higher-functioning, and since parents generally want to see their children interact with others who are on roughly the same level, camps tend to be somewhat specialized in the types of disorders they accommodate.

Parents don't always understand that, and Robyn says we need to have a broad-based idea of what the camp will be like before we enroll our children. "One of the things parents need to be aware of is that there will be children in the group who aren't exactly like their child. We do have a little bit of a range, and so sometimes – not a lot but sometimes – I will get a parent who asks, 'Why is that child in this group?' They have to understand that if they're choosing a special needs camp, their children are not going to be with 100 percent typically developing children. Even though they know that, intellectually they know that, I think sometimes initially, especially for a child who is included in a regular classroom, it's a little bit of an awakening."

Special needs camps tend to communicate with parents on a more regular basis than typical camp settings. Younger children will have a "message book" that carries information from the camp to the parents, and vice versa, on a daily basis. For older children and teens, the camp will call on a regular basis, sometimes as much as once a week, to report on progress, and parents are always able to call the camp if a situation arises that demands attention.

"I think sometimes parents don't even want that much communication. But most do. Some would like to be a fly on the wall and see how their child is doing a camp. Some are just happy for everything to be going okay," Robyn Tanne says.

It's important when dealing with a summer camp – either a day camp or a residential camp – to keep your expectations realistic. Seven weeks at a camp setting aren't going to "cure" your child's AS – nothing will do that. But if your goal is for your child to have an enjoyable experience in an environment that seems safe and understanding of his or her differences, a special needs camp might be the way to go.

If, however, your child is sensitive about his AS, and wants desperately to "fit in" with neurotypical peers, then a "mainstream" camp might be the way to go, as long as you contact the camp director when making your decision, explain the disorder and find out exactly what accommodations can be made, and how flexible the camp's staff can be in dealing with Asperger Syndrome.

Always tour the camp before enrolling your child, no matter what summer environment it might be. You'll notice the red flags for your child even a camp director won't. A neurotypical environment camp director won't know what to look for, and even the director of a special needs camp doesn't know your child nearly as well as you do. Ask for a daily schedule to find out exactly how your child will spend the day, and look for the obstacles. Take notes, and ask about each one. Don't enroll your child in any camp until each obstacle has been dealt with.

"When I'm dealing with the new parent, I'm extremely patient, almost to the point where I'm talking a little bit too much," Robyn Tanne says. "I want them to understand the choice that they're making. I want them to understand what we see as the advantage of the choice they're making. They have to feel that they're choosing an environment where there are advantages for their child. Their goals have to be the same as our goals."

Parents who can stay at home during the summer – or who can't afford the price of a day or residential camp, which can be substantial – are constantly on the lookout for day trips and activities that will keep the child with AS active. Community pools are usually a good bet (except when it rains); there are also camp programs in many towns for children who are already included in school; and some parents have banded together to hire a counselor, usually a special education teacher from a nearby school district or a special education student at a local college or university, to organize a small play group for children with autism spectrum disorders during the summer.

The good news is: there are far more options to choose from than there were even when Joshua was diagnosed in 1995. The better news: September is just around the corner.

The Principal Is Your Pal

*F*OR THE ASPERGER PARENT, NO RELA-
tionship is more complex than that with the public school
system. It is that bureaucracy that sometimes persuades parents
that private schools with staffs trained to deal with special education situations are better for their children with AS. Public
schools, with their limited budgets, state and municipal regula-
tions and responsibility to every child in the district, are not
always the most obvious suppliers of the best education for
children with AS.

Asperger parents have enough to deal with. We face the
repetition of every sentence we utter, the meltdowns, the special
interests, the food issues, the rituals, the mood swings, the lack
of eye contact, the sibling rivalry, the social skills group, the occupational therapy, the speech therapy, the medication and the repetition of every sentence we utter (or did I mention that already?).

What we really want, once we decide to place our children in an inclusive public school program, is for the school to handle the educational and social issues during the school day. That doesn't seem to be so much to ask. We're happy to handle getting the child out of bed in the morning, dressed, fed and cleaned up. We'll take care of help with homework, after-school activities, all the necessary therapies and medical appointments, care and feeding, and getting the child into bed at night so we can have a half hour of peace (hopefully) before we crawl, exhausted, into bed ourselves. We'll even make ourselves available for help during the school day if an unusual situation arises and advice is necessary. All we ask is that the school system handle the *average* days in class.

Still, sometimes it seems that is too much to ask. School systems believe we are asking for too many accommodations; sometimes, the ones that haven't heard of AS believe we are simply lax parents unable to discipline unruly children, or they think our children have ADHD and that medication should help "control" them. It can be a struggle to ask for an aide, for the kinds of therapy and accommodations our children need to thrive in a school system that is probably not prepared for the kind of challenges Asperger Syndrome offers.

Thankfully I am, in this case, *not* speaking from experience. The school system Josh attends in our New Jersey town has been as accommodating as can be since he entered the system in kindergarten. We've had to ask for special help on occasion, but no reasonable request has ever been questioned, let alone denied. Josh has worked with a paraprofessional since second grade (he is now entering seventh, and middle school, and his aide has been the same hard-working woman since third grade), has received speech therapy (until we and the school system agreed he no longer needed it) and occupational therapy through the school. His IEP meetings are a pleasure. We get the good donuts and bagels.

But I believe that part of the reason our experience has been so positive – and unusually so, according to the many parents I've interviewed and spoken with over the years – is that my wife and I have made sure *not* to take on a provocative attitude in our dealings with the schools. We don't go in, as Lori Shery often says, "with guns blazing," assuming that the system won't provide our son with what he needs unless we intimidate it into submission. Our dealings with teachers, administrators and all school officials have been cordial, and on the rare occasions when we *do* have to make noise and threaten to hold our breath until we turn blue, the people in the school system know that this is unusual, that we don't generally act that way, and something must truly be wrong, or desperately important, for us to deviate from our usual behavior. So they sit up and take notice.

"A couple of times over the years, I've had to leave a message for the director of special services or my case manager. The message was, 'This hasn't been done, it's now been X amount of time, the district is now out of compliance, and I don't think you want me to follow up on that, do you?'" says Lori. "And it gets done in a day; it's amazing. I can be tough; I can be assertive if I need to be. But if you go in there with guns blazing, forget it. You absolutely lose it, and your child loses. You can't say, 'Forget I said that; forget I called you that.'"

The frustration among Asperger parents is palpable, and you can understand how it builds. Many teachers don't understand the disorder, and see it the way the parents who give us The Look see it: we're simply not disciplining our children properly. These are behavior problems, they believe, not children with special needs. They react with impatience, with resistance, with everything up to and including disdain. They don't really see what we're dealing with, or what they have to do to make the situation work in their classrooms.

For Ellen Silva, the latest battle came when her son was assigned a teacher for the following year whom she felt would be the wrong fit. "At the end of the school year you get a teacher's name. The teacher I got has a reputation for being a yeller and a screamer. I went to the principal and said no way. At first he gave

me, 'Well let's try it, and then we'll see.' I said no. I'm not saying she's not a good teacher, but she's not the type of teacher my son needs. He needs stability. If you move him into another class, that's not going to be a good situation." Ellen understood what her son needed, held firm in her dealings with the school, didn't have to become a "difficult parent " – and got what she wanted.

Bad school situations can be systemic, from the board of education on down, or they can be specific, as specific as one teacher in a school otherwise full of helpful, caring souls. It is very important that we are allowed input about decisions on the placements our children are given in their school careers; in other words, we need to research the school system, decide which teachers we prefer our children to have, and then make our preferences known loud and clear, when necessary, and stick to our guns, although they should remain "un-ablaze" until we have run into that resistance and found ourselves backed up to a brick wall.

"You may still find it in pockets in different schools; you could have a different situation among different schools within any particular school district. From classroom to classroom," says John Masters, director of educational services for the district in Highland Park, New Jersey.

Some parents feel the problem is more pervasive than that; they maintain teachers don't understand Asperger Syndrome as a high-functioning form of autism, or as a disorder of any type. They mistake our children for those with ADD or ADHD (although some children with AS also have elements of those disorders, and that has to be addressed as well), or for behavioral problems who need to be "brought in line" or removed from class entirely.

I know of one child with AS who has been removed from his included classroom and taken to a special needs school at the expense of the local school system, because his teacher felt he "was disrupting the class, and couldn't be controlled." That is not the only incident on record; some districts are willing to spend tens of thousands of dollars a year to send one child to a special private

school. A child whose parents wanted him in an included class-room now spends an hour on a bus in each direction every day.

This does not improve the reputation of many school systems, and that is part of the problem. Another problem is that the parents who have had bad experiences with school systems (and there are plenty of them) are not timid about voicing their displeasure, which is natural. The only thing wrong with that is that every support meeting will be the first for some new Asperger parent, and the first thing he or she hears will be about difficulties with school systems. As a result, the parents whose children have recently been diagnosed end up reacting to situations before they have a chance to occur. In some school districts, those situations might never have arisen, but the "new" parents are convinced there will be a battle, so they enter their first IEP meeting with negative expectations.

Relationships between Asperger parents and school systems are incredibly complicated and need to begin with at least the possibility for mutual trust and effort to help the child. This not only serves the overall purpose – to give our children the education they deserve in the most appropriate setting possible – but also helps Asperger parents and teachers remain sane through the process, which is never an insignificant goal.

If the first information we, as Asperger parents, give those who are just now discovering what it means to raise a child with AS is that school systems are never trustworthy, will fight you tooth and nail on every point, can't be expected to make the slightest accommodation unless under duress, and only respond to aggressive, obnoxious, combative parents, we are doing those new parents a disservice. We are sending them into a very important situation for their children misinformed and ready for a battle that may not be necessary or appropriate.

It's not that we should tell people there will never be a battle, but we can't be certain that every school system will make the mistakes or have the virtues that our system does. I've seen first-time support group attendees walk in with wide eyes and walk out with expressions of abject terror because all they've heard all night is our horror stories.

We go to support group meetings, and we have conversations with friends who understand, to vent; that's natural and healthy. If we didn't let off steam and unload our burdens elsewhere, we'd probably explode before our children got to fifth grade. But when we download our "bile file" onto unsuspecting Asperger parents who are just beginning to comprehend the task before them, we aren't helping anyone.

With that sermon delivered, let me agree that some school systems do behave atrociously, some teachers are terribly misinformed or just plain rigid in their thinking, some principals don't know the difference between an autism spectrum disorder and a mental illness and some special services directors completed their training in such matters back when Hans Asperger was an obscure Austrian scientist whose work was going unrecognized because he had the awful misfortune to be working in Nazi territory during World War II. There are plenty of horror stories, and almost all of them are true. My personal experience, with speech therapists, school psychologists, principals and social workers who have actually heard of AS and know the basics about its treatment, is rare. Some parents just like to complain, and some of them are Asperger parents; the difference is that most Asperger parents have more to complain about.

Parenting is not something that can be done dispassionately and done well; we are emotional about our children; that is a natural human tendency. In our dealings with schools, we often let our emotions rule over our judgment, however, and that can be a strategic and unfortunate mistake.

In the vast majority of cases, a school system's reluctance to comply with a request for accommodations doesn't stem from the system's dislike of the child, or an emotional issue about the child's behavior. It isn't about the school system's disinterest in helping a child who has special needs.

It's about money.

"Special education can be, by nature, an adversarial process for a number of reasons. One reason involves money," special education consultant and advocate Debra Schafer says. "When parents approach their school district for services for their child, cost is one of the issues on the table. Another issue – and one that has significant impact on whether the process is adversarial – is whether the parents are treated as equal members of the IEP team. The school members of the IEP team often have more information and knowledge about the laws, terminology, processes and procedures than the parents. As a result, this can impact the parents' ability to participate equally in the process. Ultimately, this scenario raises the bar for parents in terms of becoming knowledgeable so that they remain equal participants in the process. In order for collaboration to occur, parents need to recognize that they are the "experts" on their child and must approach all interactions with their school district as such."

Advocates are one resource an inexperienced Asperger parent – or one who simply needs help in dealing with a better organized group whose goals might not be the same as the parent's – can utilize. They charge for their services, but they do help arbitrate agreements that benefit the child. They have the same kind of information the school systems have, and they have gone through the process enough times to know what the rules are, what the laws are, and where to look for information that might not fall into the area of common sense. Local support groups and the national groups' web sites, as well as psychologists, psychiatrists and local autism activism groups, can direct Asperger parents toward advocates in their areas.

However, some parents, for financial reasons or because they feel they can deal with the system effectively – and many can – choose to go it alone. My wife and I, as I've demonstrated, have not had the need for an advocate, but that is less because we're so skilled and more because the school system in our town is more progressive than many others. Of course, I think we deserve credit for moving here, since we did so specifically because Josh was about to start kindergarten, and we wanted to have access to such a school system. We did our homework, and talked to other parents (we didn't know we were Asperger parents at the time, but we did know Josh had special needs) and found out where the "better" school systems were. When it was time to move, we knew where we wanted to go.

Still, the choice of a school system isn't something everyone can count on. For one thing, not every Asperger parent is going to be financially able to move to another town with better schools, no matter how badly he or she might want to. For another, the choice of one system over another might not be dramatic enough to merit a move, nor might it get the results the child with AS needs. Most parents are going to be dealing with the school system in the town in which they live, so they have to learn the skills necessary to make that experience as successful as possible.

The first thing is to know the rules. Do research. Find out what services are possible, what services your child needs. Talk to a psychologist or psychiatrist, perhaps the doctor who first diagnosed your child's AS. Find out specifically what therapies and educational accommodations will help your child succeed in school, because these are not the same for every child with AS, and do have to be individualized (hence the term "individualized educational plan," or IEP).

Once you know what can be done, and what the ideal is for your child, you have to become the advocate. Gear yourself up, make sure you know the laws governing such matters in the state where you live, because they vary. Get yourself into full battle mode …

… and then relax. A pussycat is going to do better than a lion in most of these cases.

"I do not recommend that parents go in to an IEP meeting expecting difficulties, but rather prepared for them," says Debra Schafer. "I think one of the greatest areas of need for parents trying to maneuver through special education is applying the skills they have acquired in the business or professional arena to advocating for their child. When parents walk into a school meeting – regardless of whether it's their child's special education eligibility meeting or their fifth IEP meeting – they need to be strategic. That means having a plan, being organized, and remaining focused. Parents need to be strong communicators, which means speaking and listening. They need to know how to negotiate and mediate ... and when. Without these skills, their ability to effectively advocate for their child becomes greatly diminished. Also, parents need to recognize how their own childhood school experiences frame their ability (or lack thereof) to advocate for their child's needs."

In fact, the more aggressive, more adversarial parents can end up getting their children fewer, less effective services. Dealing from a position of emotional intensity doesn't often result in fantastic results, and parents who lose their heads in dealing with school systems alienate the very people who can help their children, while failing to maintain the cool, calm demeanor that will best accomplish the goal. They're not going to be as effective in negotiations as they would be in their business lives, which is ironic, considering how much more important these negotiations might be.

Negotiations, of course, take place in various instances: either the parents and the child study team (psychologist, case manager, social worker, teacher and others) meet for the IEP meeting to determine what special services will be necessary for the child (one is held at the time of the classification, after a diagnosis is made and then one each school year to determine what changes must be made), or when a crisis arises or either the school system or the parent feels a change must be made.

At the IEP meeting, parents must be careful never to sign anything except the (usually) state-mandated form indicating that they were present at the meeting. The IEP handed around at the meeting is not the finished form; it is the *suggested* plan that has been assembled by the child study team. Changes can, and will be made, and anything the parent feels is inappropriate should be brought up and discussed right away. Make sure the changes are made *in writing* on the form while you're sitting there, and if the system refuses to do so, do not agree to the IEP and move on to the next level of administration, even if you have to take the school system to court (over a serious lack in the IEP, not merely a twenty-minute lunch break for your child's aide).

If a crisis arises, either the child's teacher or the parent is likely to call for a meeting, either between the parent and the teacher or the parent and the principal (and in some cases, with the specialist responsible for a specific aspect of the child's IEP, like occupational or speech therapy). Again, attitude is important. Going in with a combative attitude is likely to yield less than optimum results. Be charming and friendly, but not complacent and pliant. Don't give in if something is important.

When you have the right attitude at the school meetings, it's possible you will be greeted with the same grateful smiles my wife and I see when we go to Josh's school. And you might even get the good donuts and bagels.

Baby Steps

*J*OSH STARTED THIRD GRADE IN
September 1998, and the following March, the school sent
home a notice that had my wife and me absolutely stricken with
anxiety.

"Reading Sleep-In!" it announced. "An evening of reading,
games, fun and" – here's the part that caused our abject terror –
"sleeping in the school with classmates and teachers!"

They were kidding, right? Take a nine-year-old with
Asperger Syndrome, who up until this point in his life had never
so much as been to a sleepover at a friend's house, and leave him
in a school gymnasium with forty or fifty other nine-year-old
boys and maybe five adults *for the whole night*? Surely this was
some sort of mistake. Definitely, Josh wouldn't be interested. So
we wouldn't have to worry about how many times he'd be teased
by other third graders, get into a fight with someone, start to cry

211

or drive a teacher (or worse, someone else's parent) who didn't know him to distraction in front of all his peers.

The first thing Josh said when handing me the notice was, "Can I go to this? I really want to go."

Shoot me now, the voice in my head said. I smiled at him instead, and said, "Let's wait until Mom gets home," my standard way of putting off any decision tougher than whether to make him hot dogs or macaroni and cheese for dinner.

My wife and I discussed it that night as soon as we could get the kids out of earshot, and our conclusions were unanimous: (1) this was a really bad idea and (2) Josh was going to do it anyway. This was during a year when he was having an unusually difficult time dealing with his peers, so disaster was clearly at hand. I signed up to help with the "snack" portion of the evening at ten p.m. or so, my wife signed on for breakfast the next morning (Josh had specifically barred me from staying overnight, which, to be honest, I appreciated).

On the night of the event, we packed him up with a sleeping bag (luckily, the event began after dinner, so food issues were not relevant), a pillow, his best sleeping friend (a stuffed hippo, and we made sure other kids were bringing their stuffed pals as well) and held our breath after we dropped him off at school.

We waited anxiously from seven in the evening until nine-thirty, when I could begin setting up the ten o'clock snack, and get a progress report. There had been no signs of trouble at that point, but when the kids arrived for the snack, I was dismayed to see Josh chasing classmates around, trying to hit some of them and playing too rough. I tried to stop him a few times, but he was not in complete control. I quickly contemplated taking him home …

… until another father, who knew Josh from baseball practice, sidled up to me and whispered in my ear. "Don't worry," he said. "Look. All the other boys are doing exactly the same things." And they were. So I held my breath some more, finished cleaning up the snack while the boys went off to watch a video before "bed," and went home.

Neither my wife nor I slept well that night, waiting for the phone to ring. It had been made clear to all the parents involved that any misbehavior by a child, no matter the circumstances, would mean a phone call at any time of the night to come and bring the child home. We waited all night for the phone to ring, confident only in the fact that since the school was two blocks away, we'd be able to get there quickly and remove Josh from a bad situation with a minimum of unpleasantness.

The phone never rang.

Confused by the lack of difficulty, my wife and I rose early that Sunday morning, and she went off to school warily to help with breakfast. She and Josh arrived home about an hour later, with the news that, aside from hearing some scary stories from his helpful friend that kept him awake most of the night, Josh had behaved just fine at the sleep-in, and was ready to do the whole thing again the following year.

I'm sure my wife and I exhaled at some point, but I can't remember exactly when that was.

Tell that story to a friend whose child doesn't have AS, and you'll be met with a look of utter bafflement. Of course, a nine-year-old can handle a sleepover at school for one stinkin' night; what's your problem? But to an Asperger parent, the idea of letting a child go off and spend fourteen straight hours with neurotypical peers, supervised by a handful of untrained parents, is enough to raise flop sweat on the brow and inspire a trip to the medicine cabinet for some antacid.

After that episode, we praised Josh so lavishly he thought he might be in line for that year's Nobel Peace Prize. We actually bought him a gift that day and made his favorite dinner, although that isn't terribly unusual, since he only has three dinners he's willing to eat. But it was the thought that counted. We stopped short of throwing a block party, but only after some contemplation.

The small victories, the baby steps, are the important ones for children with Asperger Syndrome. Because they have social skills difficulties and other obstacles neurotypical children don't face, each tiny achievement is occasion for celebration. Other kids might be praised or rewarded for a report card with straight "A"s or graduating from middle school into high school; our children might do those things just as well, but will also recall the day they learned to tie their shoes or ride a bicycle. Josh learned to ride a bike without training wheels on August 15, 2000, and don't think we don't recall that event every year.

"It's fascinating having a child like this," says Sharon Graebener. "To see them have such difficulties, and then those difficulties start to lessen. The people who work with them see that too. When (Max) has a great day, the aide who works with him is thrilled."

I understand that. Mrs. Gregus, the paraprofessional who helps Josh through the day, is downright exultant every time he clears a tiny hurdle, and that is one of the reasons she's been so remarkably successful with him.

It's difficult for us to recognize the achievements sometimes, because many of them come gradually. On occassions when Josh was driving me especially crazy, I have sometimes taken a moment to remember how much more frequently this happened a year ago, or two years ago, and that helped mark the amount of progress he's made. When you live with someone on a daily basis, you don't see him grow as clearly as those who only see him once in a great while.

"(Christopher) did Cub Scouts," Ellen Lemma says of her eight-year-old son. "A friend of mine, her husband is a Cub master, and they took him in. We told them about the Asperger Syndrome, and they said it's not a problem. He won the Outstanding Achievement Award for his den. He showed the most improvement from September until the end of the year. I was so overcome; I couldn't believe it. It was so great. And he had a great time."

For another parent, winning an outstanding achievement award at Cub Scouts might be occasion to ruffle the boy's hair and say, "Good job." For an Asperger parent, it is difficult not to send out formal announcements.

We are not overreacting. Celebrating our children's little victories is one of the blessings of being an Asperger parent; it gives us more reasons to applaud our children. And since it is so difficult for them to make a friend, tie a shoe, cut up a steak, write in cursive or answer the phone properly, it is that much more important to note the accomplishment and mention it to the child.

Don't be embarrassed about the baby steps when other children might have mastered a particular skill a year or two (or five) ago. Our children have to put more effort into everything (except driving us to distraction; that they do quite naturally), and their victories are harder fought than those of neurotypical children. There is no reason not to draw more attention to these small victories, because the truth is that they're not all that small.

"At the support meetings, we talk about these little victories," says Lori Shery of ASPEN. "It's important to make parents cognizant of the fact that little victories are really big victories for our children. To look at it as progress. It's very important to make a big deal. The funny thing is, once they're teenagers, they get annoyed with us. Adam, at fifteen, gets very annoyed with us when we make a big deal over any of his little victories. I still let him know that I think it's great, but he's like, 'Mom, don't embarrass me.'"

Josh and I had many a tooth and nail battle over riding his two-wheeler. For years, we would periodically take the bike to the park near our home. There he would grit his teeth, put on every possible piece of padding and body armor available to a boy that size, and climb on the bike, determined that this time would be *the* time. We both always started out with a terrific attitude and all the confidence in the world.

For the first ten minutes.

He'd climb on that seat, look ferocious, and push off with one foot. You could see the wheels in his head turning: push off on this foot, not that one, put the foot on the pedal, start pedaling, steer, look out for bumps, trees and dips in the roadway, keep pedaling!, don't look at the ground, is my helmet on tight enough?, uh-oh ... After a few seconds, if that long, down he'd go, deliberately turning the handlebars all the way to one side or another because he thought it made his "wipeout" look better. He'd lie on the ground under the bike, posing, showing off how hard he'd tried – and can we go home now?

This ritual drove me absolutely to distraction. I'd promise myself ahead of time that I wouldn't get upset, it wasn't his fault, he *wasn't doing it on purpose*, I should be a strong, supportive dad. But the fact was, my blood pressure was rising with each abortive attempt.

I wasn't angry because in some macho fantasy I saw my son taking over for Lance Armstrong, or out of embarrassment that my son couldn't ride a bike when all the other dads' kids could. It wasn't Josh's inability that angered me (and we had some doozies of scenes over the bike, I can tell you). On the contrary, I was getting more and more irritated with each try because *I knew he could do it*. On more than one occasion, when Josh wasn't thinking so hard and trying to multitask, he had ridden a two-wheel bike as early as age eight. But he couldn't do it consistently because he couldn't stop thinking about falling, and that was scaring him so severely he wouldn't keep pedaling or stay balanced.

We went through this horror show for years, and I finally resigned from the job of teaching Josh to ride a bike. For one thing, it wasn't doing either of us any good, and for another, he was getting bigger and heavier, and running beside him and the bike, holding both up while he pretended to pedal, was knocking the wind out of me in very short order. I'm not in the same shape I was in college. I'm not sure I was in that good shape *then*.

Josh, for his part, gave up on the idea. He didn't have anywhere to go anyway, he told me, and he just wasn't going to be able to do it. Case closed. Why bother, when he'd already tried?

Then, one August, Josh came home from summer camp one night and quite nonchalantly announced that he could ride a bicycle now. Three forks hit the table at the same time, and smiles broke out all around the kitchen. How did he do *that*?

In this case, fate (and more patient people than myself) intervened. There was a program for bicycle riding instruction at Josh's summer camp, and in that environment, with plenty of children his age who had exactly the same difficulty as Josh, he didn't have to worry about who was watching or whether he would fall. And the counselors were probably less apoplectic than his previous teacher. Shortly after his eleventh birthday, he got on the bike, rode it, and hasn't stopped since. One thing about riding a two-wheeler; you can't forget how. It's just like riding a bike.

The first thing we did that night was go out and buy Josh a new bicycle, the first of many. And even though it was less than two weeks after his birthday, and he had been showered with gifts by overindulgent relatives as usual, he still had a special look of pride on his face when we brought that bicycle home. He doesn't ride as much as he used to these days, because he's going through an anti-exercise phase, but he does still get on the bike every now and then, and there is never a question of ability, fear or hesitation. My son can ride a bike.

This is not an isolated case, by the way. Bicycles, the very symbol of childhood to many, can be hideous enemies to children with AS. The physical motor skills and multitasking involved can lead to chains of failure, to the extent that many children with AS are unable to ride, even with training wheels. Some can't handle a tricycle.

Ellen Lemma says one of Christopher's most recent little victories is riding a bike, and she's been ready to applaud. "I see him changing, and I see him maturing and accomplishing things that three years ago he couldn't do. It's not just maturation; it's also the therapies and everything. He was riding a bike and he couldn't do that before. He's having a little trouble, but he's trying.

And that's something that he wouldn't have tried two years ago. He even fell off the bike, and he was mad, but he got back on. It makes you look at things that other parents would take for granted and say, 'Wow, look at that.' I told him, 'I'm really proud of you, and you tried.'"

Sometimes, the little victories come in places you don't expect them, and can't see them coming. The first time your child doesn't come down the stairs three times to get tucked in is a tiny victory, even if it's best not to celebrate that one, for fear the child might think you don't like spending bedtime with him. The first time he doesn't need help getting into or out of the shower (and in all likelihood, spends a half hour under the water without someone to stop him) is a little victory. Trying a new food is a huge achievement, even if he doesn't end up adding it to his menu. Bringing in the mail without being asked. Noticing that a conversation is going on when he enters the room, and not interrupting immediately. Recognizing tone of voice or body language. I remember the first time Josh looked at me and said, "That's sarcasm, isn't it?" In my family, that is a tremendous little victory. But maybe his greatest accomplishment has been playing video games.

In 1997, when Josh was eight years old, we bought him a Nintendo 64 game console. We were the only parents in the history of America to buy their child a video game system because they thought it would be good for him.

It was a difficult school year for him, and the other children were starting to notice that Josh wasn't very much like them. He was being teased aggressively for the first time, and not reacting well. There had also been incidents on the playground during recess. We hadn't yet been called to see the principal, but that was probably on the horizon.

Josh told me one night that he didn't have any friends, and while I had probably known that already, it had never been articulated quite that bluntly before. My wife and I discussed it at length, feeling that much of his current problems could be tied to

Josh's feelings that the other children didn't like him and that he didn't know how to find common ground.

He was going to social skills group once a week during this period, and it was helping with the nuts and bolts of interaction, like starting a conversation and understanding body language. But Josh simply didn't have anything to talk about that the other kids his age wanted to hear.

Seizing the opportunity, we decided to get him the video game. After all, every eight-year-old boy in the country wanted one, plenty had one, and if there was ever a subject matter that would engage Josh and give him an opening, it was that. Besides, having a Nintendo unit in the house meant other children would be coming over after school to play. So having the newest, coolest one could at least give Josh some status on the playground. Word of such things gets around quickly.

Being Josh, he bristled initially (after the initial jubilation at the Holy Grail of Chanukah gifts) at the prospect of having to play video games against *other people*. He believed that other people came to our house to watch *him* play video games. As the guidance counselor at his primary school once told us, "Josh doesn't want friends. He wants cast members." But once he became somewhat proficient at the game or two he had gotten to play, he felt ready to take on peers.

Within a few months, he had played against five of his class-mates, two of them repeat visitors. There was a sneaking suspicion that a couple of the boys had come over after school to play with the video game and not our son, but that was all right in the beginning. To this day, he can play video games (now in three different formats) with a steady stream of friends, and he can discuss them (at great length) with kids his own age – even those whose names he has trouble remembering when he gets home from school.

"He was telling me about his friends, and they talk about (video games) at school," Ellen Lemma says of eight-year-old Christopher. "He tells me what level he got to, and it's socially acceptable. Our kids end up becoming so good at these games – he's so intent on getting to that next level, he'll play for hours if I let him. He even handled losing one of his games pretty well. I said, 'it's a forty-dollar game and you have to save up your money and get a new one.' He let it go; he's playing the other games, and it's not that important. I've got to limit him because he won't do other things."

As a way to improve social skills per se, I can't recommend Game Cube or PlayStation 2 ("PS2," Josh corrects me) for children with AS. But as a way to break the ice, as a topic of conversation, I can say that boys, especially, find it universally acceptable. Josh will often call – or be called by – friends to ask a question about a particularly difficult passage. It's not much, but it's a start.

The baby steps are the tiny victories our children manage in the course of an average day. Because they do have Asperger Syndrome, there can be more of these moments in their lives than there might be in the lives of their neurotypical peers. It gives us and our children more opportunities to celebrate achievement. Is that a bad thing?

Lighten up on Yourself

YOU MAY HAVE NOTICED THAT throughout this book, I have not painted a picture of myself as the perfect Asperger parent. I have thrown my own temper tantrums, wielded sarcasm as a weapon, failed to take a Cleansing Breath when an entire tank of oxygen could have been inhaled, lost control and been slow on the uptake at various times during Josh's upbringing, which is still very much in progress.

Of course, there are those who know me who will read this book and conclude that I'm being too easy on myself, but that's another story entirely.

I'm willing to bet there have been times when you, too, didn't measure up to your own high standards of Asperger parenting. You snapped at an innocent comment, lost your temper when an explanation would have been more appropriate, got exasperated because you didn't know the answer to the one hun-

221

dredth question of the hour, didn't prepare well enough for an IEP meeting, alienated a teacher and snapped at your spouse who just walked in the door from work and had the nerve to ask how things were going.

We both need to lighten up on ourselves. Parents are human beings, like it or not, and it's not reasonable to expect anything resembling perfection from us. Asperger parents, given the added challenges we face in the course of a day, sometimes feel we should be awarded a gold medal, at the very least, for making it through another twenty-four hours. Usually what we get is an engraved invitation to clean up the kitchen and help with homework.

This isn't about forgiving; it's about relaxation. It's not about escaping AS; it's about learning to enjoy it more, or at least mind it less. This is about not taking seriously the things that aren't serious, and being very serious about the things that actually require attention. Don't sweat the small stuff – but guess what, it's not all small stuff.

We need to take a step back every once in a while and consider the scope of what we're trying to accomplish. It's not enough to try and navigate a child through the complex, Kafkaesque world our peers contend with; we have to contend with a disorder that sees nothing the way everyone else – and in most cases, we belong to "everyone else" – sees it. We have to learn to recognize that while everything our children do has a tinge of AS to it, not everything is a result of the disorder. Empathy, rather than sympathy, is the most important thing we can offer our children, because it will help us see the world through their eyes, and that means we can be more understanding about the things they do.

None of this is easy, particularly since our children's capacity for empathy in return is limited. They have difficulty seeing the other person's side of the story, because there are times they have difficulty noticing there is another person.

What's important? Lightening up is important. That means trying to smile more often than you grimace. Attempting to see the tiny signs of progress, and not the tremendous-seeming obstacles. Doing what you can to make your child see the wonder that is inside her and not the difficulties the outside world seems so intent on providing.

What we're talking about is learning what is important and what can slide by. You need to be alert, because an AS meltdown or a ticklish situation with a peer could crop up at any time. But you also need to understand that there are times when you just sit back and let it happen, and stop worrying for a moment or two.

It sounds like it should be easy, right? You love your child, and you help her through many of the challenges in an average day. You want her to be happy, you don't want her to feel stressed out and concerned that you're going to tell her at any moment that she's doing something wrong. You don't need to add anxiety to a disorder that's already enough to deal with. So you should be able to just let your child live her life every once in a while.

The problem is, it's not as simple as all that. We Asperger parents are so attuned to watching our children's every move, to anticipating every possible situation and warding off all that can go wrong, that we have a hard time disengaging that impulse when it isn't essential. Your son's best friend may not care – or notice – that he is stimming wildly while they play their video game, but you're going to try to stop him anyway. You may not even care that your child insists on having carrots with every meal, but after a while, you're going to protest carrots with the pancakes on a Sunday morning.

It's not that we're all obsessive-compulsive personalities; it's not that we can't ever see anything in our lives but our children with AS. We've simply managed – through necessity, since it is an essential tool of Asperger parenting – to condition our responses. Remember the chapter in your tenth-grade science book about Pavlov's dog? How the scientist had repeated the procedure of ringing a bell and then giving his dog a treat to the point that the dog began to drool whenever a bell rang? That is precisely what we do to ourselves. We practice our Asperger parenting skills over and over, making sure we're watching over *everything*, because we know that some of these situations are going to be important, and some will be critical. We don't ever know when the critical ones will be coming, so we treat each successive situation that our children encounter as important and serious. By the time we're practiced enough to be very good at anticipation, we've also trained ourselves so thoroughly that we don't always see the truth, which is that some of these situations are trivial and momentary, and won't be remembered in five minutes. The lasting effect on our children's lives in many cases will be absolutely nothing.

"There are some youngsters with Asperger Syndrome whose parents have a dash of social phobias themselves, and I think it's extraordinarily difficult under those situations," says Dr. Jed Baker. "I have seen that maybe a third of the time, anecdotally. That's what Hans Asperger said, that there is sometimes a dash of the disorder in fathers of individuals with AS. But just because you think about AS doesn't mean you have it. For example, medical students often worry that they have every disease they're reading about, when in fact they don't."

This complicates matters, because that means a decent percentage of Asperger parents will find themselves reacting with a touch of the obsession to detail that our children exhibit. And that makes it a degree harder to relax in any social situation, particularly one involving your child with AS.

"I'm trying to back off, and even if he has a bad day, part of me says, 'OK, Max, that's your life. I'll try and do everything I can for you,'" says Sharon Graebener. "That's the part I'm having the hardest time with, making Max feel responsible for his own life. If you have homework, it's your homework."

Naturally, children who are used to having a parent, teacher or aide hovering over them at any given moment of the day are going to find less supervision unusual. Some children with AS will react with astonishment the first time a parent doesn't swoop in and negotiate a dispute with a sibling. Others won't notice. But the parent, assuming no enormous incident ensues, might have an eye-opening experience.

Visiting Josh's third-grade class, my wife might have been cringing just a little at the amount of self-stimming behavior Josh was doing. His hands were on his face, his eyes rolling back in his head, his high-pitched humming noticeable from her seat in the row behind him. Surely, the other children in the class were going to protest to the teacher, tease him later on the playground, or otherwise have a negative reaction to these antics. She prepared herself to step in and defuse the situation before it would get worse.

But she had no time. The girl sitting next to Josh, after a few minutes of stimming, reached over and touched him lightly on the arm. "Josh," she said, "cut it out." Josh stopped, nodded, and got back to the writing on his desk.

My wife was impressed; that girl must be a particularly understanding type, she figured. But after the boy on Josh's other side stopped a second round of stimming, and the other children in the class simply failed to notice anything out of the ordinary, she reached a new understanding: these kids had known our son and his AS for four years, and they *didn't care*. It didn't faze them that his behavior wasn't like their own. He was Josh, and that's what Josh does. It didn't seem to be anything even worthy of comment to them.

Not every potential slight or conflict is that easy to avoid, but the fact that a situation can be avoided *without our intervention* can be something of a revelation to the Asperger parent. And once that revelation has been absorbed, it can open doors to us we had never expected: the fabled Five Minutes Off, which many in our ranks had scoffed would never be achieved in our lifetimes.

Giving yourself permission to take Five Minutes Off is a huge step for an Asperger parent. It means that, while we're still on call 24/7, we don't have to be *on duty* every second of every day. That's a mind-stretching difference, and one that should not be taken lightly. If our children can survive, even thrive, without us for short periods of time, that must mean we can have time to devote to the rest of our lives, which is something many Asperger parents have not even considered for years.

The freeing effect can be intoxicating.

It's helpful for the child as well. When it's possible to show your child you have enough confidence to let her work out a small problem, or leave her alone in the house (assuming the child is responsible and old enough) for a few minutes, the boost of self-confidence can be significant. It can demonstrate to your child that although you know her AS does cause her some difficulties, you are secure enough in her abilities to trust her with a fraction of the responsibility for her actions and her welfare. It's a subtle concept, and one that some children with AS might need to have explained, but it is important.

The difficult part, for some parents, is being able to let go. One Asperger mother I spoke to (who asked not to be identified) said she knows she should be letting her son have more freedom. She acknowledges he's ready for it, but she has a very hard time disengaging from her Supermom mode.

"I've spent so much time watching (my son) like a hawk," she says. "I don't know how to stop. And I can tell he knows I'm watching; he'll sometimes turn around and say to me, 'Don't worry, Mom, I'm all right.' It's not his problem; it's mine."

Although it seems logical, this problem is not helped by the fact that the child is in school most of the day. Asperger parents have a higher level of anxiety during the school day, waiting for the phone to ring with a problem, than most parents, and when the day is over, the child comes home to a parent (or two) who is more than interested in how the school day went.

Josh often comes stomping through the front door (that's just the way he walks) and tries as quickly as possible to get upstairs to his room before he's subjected to the Third Degree by his jailer (that's me) on how things went at school today. Parents, especially Asperger parents, can be so *annoying* when you're just barely a teenager.

This problem is partially solved when Mrs. Gregus, the paraprofessional who stays with Josh through his school day, reports in her notebook, which we make sure is in Josh's backpack every day. She'll let us know when things are a little rough, but lately (for the past year or so), she's had almost uniformly positive reports. It helps me to relax just a little bit.

Besides, there's another child in the house to obsess over. Eve, about to turn ten, requires attention, if not in the same way (and possibly not to the same degree, although that is debatable) that Josh does. The fact is, when they get home from school, it is usually Eve, and not Josh, who needs attention about her day and her homework. Also, she is more likely to be going outside to play, while Josh will probably hole up in his room and hunker down with the video games after he finishes his homework. (We had good intentions with that video game system, but we created a monster.)

One thing about children with Asperger Syndrome: they can be awfully good at amusing themselves. The autism spectrum allows for a wide range of activity going on at all times in their minds, and while that doesn't give a parent the excuse to go off and never engage the child in activity or conversation, it does allow both parent and child the occasional moment to relax and be themselves.

Lightening up is simply a process of relaxing your grip on the arms of your chair, un-gritting your teeth, and letting out your breath for the first time in uncounted months. It's the realization that things aren't always going to be desperate, times aren't always hard and challenges don't present themselves every ten minutes; it just feels that way. It is a way to recognize your effort and the results it has produced. It is the best reward you can have, because it comes with progress for your child, and now both of you can relax for a minute or two.

That may seem simple, and it may seem small. To non-Asperger parents, it might even appear insignificant. It is none of those things. Children with AS require more attention naturally, and our inclination, once we have heard the diagnosis and researched the condition, is to provide that attention, sometimes to the point of near-obsession (after all, they didn't come by their AS at the mall). We are a perfect match, Asperger parents and our children, and that means that sometimes neither one of us knows how to change.

First, we should celebrate. Those tiny victories we discussed have blossomed into something that has actually improved the quality of life in the family. That is an enormous accomplishment, and should never go unnoticed.

Then, as with everything else, we need to discuss it. Children with AS need to be reassured that just because Mom or Dad isn't going to cut up their meat for them, it doesn't mean we're giving up on the whole idea of child care. It means they've acquired a new skill, and we're letting them use it. If that skill happens to be hanging out in a room with a friend for a half hour without supervision, all the better.

We parents have been planning for years around that moment when we might have some time to ourselves. Some of us take up painting, or gardening, or read that book that's been sitting on the bed stand since 1997. Others *write* that book that's been in their minds since around the same time. You are currently reading one of them.

Consider this an early rehearsal for the really big moment: when the child with AS is no longer a child.

You'll Always Be an Asperger Parent

ROBIN WILLIAMS ONCE SAID THAT you have two fantasies about your child while he's growing up: one in which he stands in front of a podium and thanks the Nobel Institute, and another where his main form of communication is, "You want fries with that?"

Welcome to the wonderful world of Asperger parenting for an adult. Children, oddly enough, tend to grow up at some point, and when they do, they inevitably try to lead their own lives, something that can leave even the parent of a neurotypical child stunned and confused. Add to that situation the compounded challenges of a person with Asperger Syndrome, and the scenario, like so many others we've seen, becomes complicated by geometric degrees.

You didn't think this was going to get any easier as your child got older, did you?

Remember: you'll *always* be an Asperger parent. Parenting, by definition, is not a job that ever ends and for us, the challenges will continue well into our children's adulthood. Support groups for both adults with AS and their families have formed around the country, and more information about the differences of being an adult with an autism spectrum disorder is becoming available every day.

Our children tend to do quite well academically in included school environments, all the way through high school. This isn't true of every child with AS, but it is quite common. However, sometimes problems surface when the young adult is making the transition from high school to college, or the first job after graduating from school.

Some Asperger parents, even those with advanced degrees and careers in the professions, find that the organizational and emotional issues connected with going to college would be too much for their children with AS to handle. This realization takes some adjustment, as we sometimes have to shelve the hopes and dreams we've had since our children were born.

"We need to look ahead," says Lori Shery. "My expectations adjusted, and this is how they adjusted. We started out thinking, well, certainly he'll go to a four-year college, a decent school if not Harvard. And he'll get a job in some kind of profession. Now that Adam is in high school, and I have to be more realistic, and I talk to other parents who've been there and done that and maybe their children are nineteen or twenty as opposed to thirty-five or forty (because they wouldn't have gotten services), we're starting to realize that he's very bright and he gets good grades but that doesn't mean he can be successful in college. It's too early to tell. I know of too many of our children who flunked out the first semester. It's mainly because they couldn't get organized, they couldn't get themselves up to go to class; they were on their own and didn't know how to be."

Joshua, who is just starting middle school, is not the most organized person who ever lived, either. He still needs the help of an aide to get him from place to place in school, make sure his homework comes home, and that he understands the assignment before he leaves class. He gets very good grades, but we don't yet have an indication of whether he'll be able to move on after high school (although he says he wants to follow in his father's footsteps and go to Rutgers). It's too early to know.

Maggie Casciato, whose son Tom is twenty-two years old, helped him get a job in the office where she works as an accountant. College would have been too difficult for him, she says, and he actually stayed in high school an extra year, although his grades were adequate to merit graduation after his senior year.

"There were some good experiences (in high school) until it was time to do transition. That was a real problem," Maggie says. "Our town didn't do it very well. They're supposed to plan for work experience outside of school, but they never got around to it. They gave him a job in the school, and it was a good job. They even paid him for it. He was an aide in the library, helping kids do research on the Internet. But as far as working outside of school in the community, they never did it. I knew it was in his ITP, the transition plan, and when it came time to graduate, I said, 'you still haven't done this, and I don't think he should graduate until you complete his transition plan.' So they grudgingly agreed, and kept him on another year. He didn't go to class, but he did work with a school-provided aide for an extra year."

Many people with AS have attended and graduated from colleges all over the country. Now that each of us has seen the disorder and learned to recognize it, we probably realize which students in our graduating classes had AS and didn't know it at the time. But college – particularly when the student is living away from home – presents a wealth of challenges, perhaps the least of which is the actual studying.

The late teenage years also often include an introduction to driving a vehicle, always a stressful and exciting time for the young adult, and a worrisome time for the parents. With AS, attention to multitasking and concentration on the road can become issues. Many people with Asperger Syndrome are driving vehicles on the road every day, which is something we might want to consider the next time we're cursing another driver out under our breath.

Living away from home for the first time can be an enormous challenge for a person with Asperger Syndrome. Just keeping track of laundry can either become an obsession, or lie undone for weeks, even months, at a time. Eating habits become more difficult to maintain, or to break. Time management is often a large issue.

In many cases, the student with AS doesn't finish school, or chooses not to attend college at all. Some Asperger parents feel that a workable alternative is a year or two at a community college to see if a four-year course will be appropriate, or application to a college or university close enough to home so that the student can commute to school and avoid at least some of the difficulties living on campus can present.

Others leave high school and immediately go to work, even if they don't have a clear plan of action or a particular career path they want to pursue.

"He still isn't sure what it is he wants to do," Maggie Casciato says of Tom. "He took a couple of courses at the local community college. But Tom's the type of kid who, if he doesn't see an immediate result, just isn't interested. If you could tell him, 'you take this class, and next week you'll get a job paying 30,000 dollars,' he would do it, but the idea of going to school and just taking general English, he didn't see the use of it. With the help of a job coach provided by the Bureau of Rehabilitation Services, he did get a job in my office."

Neuropsychologist Dr. Elizabeth Roberts says that in some ways the special focused interest many people with AS have can be a help when they begin thinking about a career. "To me, the saving thing could be a hobby that has vocational implications that the kid has started doing in high school, which can give him an identity or guide or career path," she says. "One kid I knew who had Asperger Syndrome compiled a huge fund of information about kayaks. He ended up volunteering at this kayak store, and he became indispensible to them."

Adults with AS often find themselves in jobs that don't require a lot of interaction with other workers. Computer whizzes can sometimes find a wonderful outlet, working on a computer console and not having to worry about saying the wrong thing or looking the wrong way to others. Maggie Casciato's son works in a company mailroom, and he has a very set routine, which he is reluctant to change. This can sometimes be a problem in an office environment, where everything can't be counted on to stay the same every single day.

"Currently, he's very rigid regarding what he does at work, and he has a certain routine. If you ask him not to do a certain task now, but to do something else instead, he gets very flustered and might even refuse to do it," Maggie reports. "I've seen him or heard him be a little quick, a little short. Some bosses wouldn't put up with it, I know. They tolerate his eccentricities, and they like him. He's a nice kid and has a great sense of humor. The people he works with have learned to get along with him. He's very fortunate."

It was a disappointment to Maggie and her husband when Tom opted not to go to college, although they understood the decision. She says that the town in which she lives boasts more than half their graduating high school seniors going to a four-year college. Tom went to a community college for a while, but dropped out after becoming frustrated with the courses he was studying.

"My husband and I are both college educated and we assumed our kids would be doing the same thing," Maggie says. "You ache. There's an ache that says, 'that will not be my son.' It's partially academic. He has his strength, which is maybe English, but not math or science. He can hear people at work who have degrees in architecture, and correct their grammar. He loves words and puns. I don't believe about (people with AS) not getting puns, because Tom does. He would probably be able to struggle through college as a C student."

Maggie lives near Yale University, and has availed herself of the information available at the Yale Child Study Center and the university libraries. She recognizes some students at the Ivy League school whom she believes have AS, and others who know they do, and continue to study. An academic environment can sometimes be more welcoming to those with "eccentricities" than a work environment. Intelligent students who do well in high school and sometimes in college end up being employed in work that doesn't take into account their studies, mainly because of their difficulties with the social aspects of the work environment.

"There's a very high-functioning kid who graduated from Yale who used to work part-time at the Yale Child Study Center. He's spoken at lots of national conventions," she says. "He calls it 'malemployment.' Not unemployment. It's true. Those who have college degrees are working in pizza places and grocery stores. No matter what their academic background is, they can't keep a job because they can't fit the social profile they need to hold onto a job. So Tom has pointed out, 'if I had gone to college, I'd still be in the same situation I am today.' Tragic, but true. There are some kids who succeed in holding full-time jobs but mainly it's because of connections, or because it's a job that doesn't require that they socialize. They work on computers all day."

Once in a work environment, other challenges present themselves to adults with AS. Dating is difficult for anyone, and for those whose social skills are questionable, or at least an area of low self-confidence, it can be too daunting to even attempt. Some adults with AS decide to stay out of the dating scene, although they do want to find a mate. Others venture out with the friends they have from school or work, but find the competitive social environment of dating too difficult to continue.

Blind dates are sometimes an alternative, if friends or family know a compatible person for the adult with AS to date. But it's never easy, and there's remarkably little we as Asperger parents can do, other than provide support and encouragement. If our children, no matter what age, are still living in our home, we can try to point out ways to prepare for social situations and make sure they are practicing social skills. Beyond that, our options begin to narrow.

The decision for a young adult with Asperger Syndrome to move out of the family home is a very significant one, to begin with. If the adult with AS feels confident enough to find an apartment or another home, it should be seen as a positive sign of confidence and ambition. But each circumstance will be different, and sometimes, parents and children who disagree throughout the teenage years might also run into serious conflicts regarding this extremely large life step.

Some of our children, after all, are not prepared – financially, socially or in terms of their organizational and life skills – to live on their own. And when they believe they are ready, we may not agree. An objective observer, like a therapist or social worker, might be the right person to mediate such a disagreement and help the parties come to terms with the practical aspects of the move.

Roommates, if the person with AS has friends who are interested in living with her, might be a worthwhile compromise. Having responsible people – not responsible for the person, but at least able to monitor her progress and avoid serious missteps – in the same living quarters can ease tensions and calm both the Asperger parents, who are often worried about impending disasters they see on the horizon, and the person with AS herself. Although her self-confidence might be high, her ability to adapt to new situations is probably, at least a little, questionable.

Some adults with AS, unfortunately, won't ever be able to live on their own. Hopefully, their parents will have enough prior notice, through examinations and opinions from professionals through the years, to prepare for a time when their children will not have the parents' home to use any longer.

"What we're really doing is preparing for the day we die," Dennis Debbaudt says. "Now all our kids are on their own. And the insurance people will tell you that (they will) be for about thirty-five years. New parents don't want to think about that. They think they're immortal. They are not prepared to think about that."

Financial planning for such a time is essential. Adults with autism spectrum disorders who do not function on a high enough level to live alone, or even with one other person, sometimes have to find assisted living facilities. The time after the trauma of a parent's death is not the time to be faced with the task of finding funds to pay for something as expensive (and life-changing) as that. Even Asperger parents who are sure their children will never attend college might consider putting money in their name every month into a college-type fund or into life insurance policies for themselves, with the child who has AS as the beneficiary.

It's not all as gruesome as it sounds; many individuals with Asperger Syndrome are very high-functioning, and need more direction, rather than flat-out living assistance. Hopefully, we provide that through the skills of Asperger parenting we learn over the years. But once our children with AS become adults with AS, much of the parenting has been done. We exist then to offer emotional and (when necessary and possible) financial support, to help raise our children's level of self-esteem, and to sit back a little and watch the amazing progress they are often capable of making. Life affords us these opportunities sometimes, and we, more than most parents, have the ability and the training to appreciate them.

After all, you're going to be an Asperger parent forever. You might as well focus on the bright side of the deal. As my wife often says of Josh, "Some day, he's going to be a terrific adult."

Hans Across America

*T*HERE IS A REMARKABLE NETWORK OF people out there. People who understand what you go through in an average day, people who can nod in recognition and smile at a situation it would take you a half hour to explain to anyone else.

For the estimated hundreds of thousands (if not millions) of people in the country who have Asperger Syndrome, one thing is indisputable: there are twice as many parents. And in the wild ride my family has been on these past seven years (and will remain on for the rest of our lives), we have run into a great number of those who share the experience, and can relate to it.

But this isn't an exclusive club. Friends of ours (in fact, the very people who were shocked at my behavior in the first chapter) understand a good deal about AS now, and don't need the reams of explanation a novice would. They can smile and nod because they have been around Josh enough to recognize the pattern; they can come to our house and speculate about someone they know who may be an Asperger parent and doesn't know it yet. They "get it."

Too often, Asperger parents are so besieged by their daily battles with the disorder and (more to the point) the ignorance about it, that we sometimes adopt an "us-against-them" attitude toward the rest of civilization. People are branded into two categories: there are "us" – those who have Asperger Syndrome in their lives – and everyone else. "Everyone else" is usually characterized as ambivalent, if not hostile, to "us."

It doesn't have to be that way. Part of what we need to do is to welcome "everyone else" into the "us" fold. We have to educate, sure, but we also need to recognize and include those whose children are not on the autism spectrum, but who want to understand and possibly to help. In our Ambassadorship to the Principality of Asperger Syndrome, we need to have open borders, to accept our neighbors and friends, and to allow for the possibility that they might not want to wage war with us.

For every sitcom joke about children on Ritalin, there is a dedicated teacher or administrator who is truly fascinated by our children and wants to help them get the education they need and are entitled to. For every purveyor of The Look or The Mope, there is someone who is willing to smile at the small triumphs and participate when things aren't quite the way we'd like them to be.

Welcome them; welcome them.

Friends and family really can understand what we have come to learn. Keep in mind: we *were* part of "everyone else" before our children were diagnosed; there was a time, hard as it is to remember, when the name "Asperger Syndrome" was just as likely to be thought of as an off-color joke as a possible reason our children were behaving differently than their peers.

Does that mean there aren't people who think we're simply bad parents, or our children are coddled and badly behaved? Of course not; there will always be those who refuse to wrap their minds around an idea they haven't considered before. Some people are stupid. You can use any politically correct label you like ("logic impaired;" "mentally ungigantic"), but it will continue to be true. Some people are narrow-minded and others are simply mean, and want to make fun of anything that isn't, well, them.

I have spent a good deal of energy and effort considering those people, and I have come to a hard-fought and well-considered conclusion: I don't have enough time on this earth to deal with them. I have enough to do.

Instead, I concentrate on the other two categories of "everyone else": those who want to understand, and those who don't know there's something to understand yet. For the first group, there are web sites, books (hopefully this one included) and periodicals that cover the topic and provide basic education. I can explain as far as I understand, but that is limited. My son's experiences won't equal yours, and no matter how much one reads and talks to others, there will always be plenty more that isn't absorbed or remembered. I have to try to take better notes.

For the second group, there must be some drum-beating, twenty-first-century style. We have to make a concerted effort to increase the amount of press coverage and information available on AS, particularly among the general population, where there are countless Asperger parents who have not yet had the disorder explained to them and are still despairing at the differences between their children and neurotypical children, and don't know why. When we didn't know why, we were considerably more frantic than we are now. Only the mass media, including the Internet, can get the word out efficiently. We have to scream from the rooftops as loudly and as often as we can.

The other thing that is seriously lacking in the autism spectrum community is cohesiveness. Each group whose members represent one aspect of the spectrum seems to be at odds with all the rest. As a result, we move toward the same goal from so many different directions that we all end up meeting in the middle and tussling over tiny spoils.

One group of Asperger parents whose children are toddlers won't communicate with another whose children are now adults and teens. Parents whose children are not high-functioning see themselves at odds with those whose kids have a higher level of social interaction. Those whose children have AS fail to join with others on the spectrum to lobby for research, funding and changes in laws that have been overdue for decades. We spend so much time arguing with each other that the rest of the world is perfectly happy to leave us to our petty disagreements and go about its business. Very little gets done in comparison to what could be, because there is distrust, ambivalence and, in some cases, downright animosity among groups whose members are all in the same very large boat that is the autism spectrum. This has to change.

Individually, Asperger parents need to do the impossible: increase their effort while they relax their intensity. Yes, we're called upon to do the work of at least two parents apiece because our children require more than their neurotypical peers. Yes, we have a good deal more responsibility than most in our school districts, and we have both medical and social issues to consider as well. Yes, we have to get involved in the community, push for an overall understanding of what our children need and what they most certainly don't need, and we have to unite with each other and with those who haven't yet heard of Hans Asperger and the disorder he was perceptive enough to notice.

At the same time, however, we need to stop grinding our teeth and take life a little more as it comes. One of the reasons the cliché of a hyperventilating, overbearing parent of a child with a mysterious disability no one can notice is becoming popular in bad television programs and movies is that it is often true. Too often, we enter situations (understandably enough) with "guns a-blazing," to quote the philosopher, when maybe we'd get better results with a smile and a lollypop.

We need to give ourselves a break, too. We're never going to meet the high standards AS sets for us, because no parent on this planet will ever be able to meet every situation perfectly. We have to train ourselves to see the bright side, to notice the little victories and applaud them, both for ourselves and for our children. We have to take our little vacations, even if they're only for five minutes at a time, because one of our responsibilities is not to go crazy. We have to maintain our sanity, our sense of humor and our patience (whatever we have of it), because we're going to need every single bit of each.

One last Josh story: As I've mentioned, his diet has been somewhat, let's say, limited, particularly in the area of dinner entrees. Fried chicken, hot dogs, macaroni and cheese, pasta. That's about it.

The other day, out of nowhere, he asked me why I was changing the way I eat and I explained that I need to lose some weight, and that's how I'm going about it. Josh thought about it for a while, and started a conversation – on his own – about his own eating habits. Why they are the way they are and what could be done about it.

That night, as per our earlier conversation, he ate an entire piece of barbecued chicken (prepared on our grill) and – best of all – a salad consisting of lettuce, carrots and celery. My wife and I told Josh how proud we were of him for taking that step, and the next night, he had the salad again. He's not going to slide back, he says. And he says there will be more steps taken to add foods to his diet.

You see? There is hope, after all.

Notes

The following people were interviewed by the author personally, and the quotes attributed to them were taken directly from those interviews:

Dr. Jed Baker, February and May 2002;

Margaret Casciato, March 2002;

Dennis Debbaudt, February 2002;

Sharon Graebener, January 2002;

Ellen Lemma, December 2001 and June 2002;

John Masters, January 2002;

Elizabeth Roberts, PSYD, July 2002;

Debra Schafer, February 2002;

Lori Shery, December 2001 and January 2002;

Ellen Silva, March 2002;

Robyn Tanne, April 2002.

Michael Levine's Ambassador Theory
is quoted with his permission.

The author extends his deepest appreciation to all the above, as their insights and comments made this book possible. His apologies to all those who were subjected to interviews twice because his tape recorder decided to be unreasonable. All of those interviewed were extremely generous with their time, their experiences and their patience – the true sign of an Asperger parent (even those who, technically, are not).

In the preparation of this book, the following web sites were invaluable:

www.aspennj.org

www.asperger.net

www.njcosac.org

www.asperger.org

www.udel.edu/bkirby/asperger/

www.aspie.org/

http://amug.org/~a203/

http://www.faaas.org/

They are all very helpful, and worth your time. And they are all free. For the article described in this book about Josh and Asperger Syndrome, go to:

http://www.usaweekend.com/99_issues/9ninety718/
9ninety718family.html

or contact *USA Weekend* for a copy of the July 18, 1999, issue.